Life With ADHD

PROVEN AND EFFECTIVE ADHD COPING STRATEGIES FOR REAL LIFE

Peter Jaksa, Ph.D.

Attention Publishing

CHICAGO, ILLINOIS

Peter Jaksa/Attention Publishing

30 North Michigan Avenue, Suite 908

Chicago, IL 60602

www.addcenters.com

Book Layout ©2017 BookDesignTemplates.com

Life With ADHD/ Peter Jaksa, Ph.D. —1st ed.

ISBN 978-1-7349923-1-1

For all people with ADHD

The only consistent thing about ADHD is inconsistency.

—ANONYMOUS

My thoughts are like butterflies.
They are beautiful, but they fly away.

—ANONYMOUS

It is better to be high-spirited even though
one makes more mistakes, than to be
narrow-minded and all too prudent.

–VINCENT VAN GOGH

Contents

Introduction..7

1 My Personal Journey (Short Version) 9

2. What Is ADHD?..17

3. Multimodal Management of ADHD.............................31

4. Medication Management and ADHD 45

5. Pay Attention! Concentration and Focusing 57

6. Get Going! Reducing Procrastination.........................65

7. Don't Forget! Memory Management Tools..................75

8. De-clutter Your Home and Work Environment 83

9. Improve Time Management....................................87

10. ADHD and Relationships 97

11. Parenting a Child With ADHD..............................103

12. Succeeding In College With ADHD 111

13. Finding a Job That Works For You..........................121

14. Tone Down Impulsivity and Hyperactivity.............127

15. ADHD and Addictions...131

16. Self-Esteem and ADHD 143

17. Living Happily and Well With ADHD.....................149

Bibliography...157

Peter Jaksa

Introduction

I BECAME AN ADHD specialist in 1985, the year I was first licensed as a clinical psychologist. Since then I have worked with thousands of people with ADHD of all ages, from a wide variety of backgrounds, engaged in a very wide variety of jobs and occupations. I have had the opportunity to work with people with ADHD from every continent except Antarctica.

Those experiences have, I believe, provided me with a good understanding of the biology of ADHD and how it affects people's lives. Living with ADHD on a personal level, as an adult with ADHD, has also contributed immensely to my understanding.

This book is written for any person with an interest in information about ADHD and proven, practical ways to manage it. In particular it may resonate with adults with ADHD who too often have been bombarded with negative messages about their behavior and their biology since they were children. To them I have two basic messages. First, you are not "broken." And second, ADHD is behavior that can be managed well.

One very important part of my professional work as a psychologist, writer, and speaker, is to dispel many of the negative stereotypes and misconceptions about ADHD. I have seen firsthand, and far too often, how these stereotypes can be destructive on so many levels.

This is not to say that ADHD biology never causes problems or challenges. It can and it does -- for many people, to different degrees, at certain points in their lives. There is nothing fun or productive about being too distracted, procrastinating too much, or being too disorganized.

On the other hand, what is essential to understand is that with the right set of strategies and tools these behaviors (excessive distractibility, procrastination, poor organization, etc.) can be managed well.

Beyond some introductory explanations, theories, and ideas discussed in Chapter 2 ("What Is ADHD?"), the majority of this book is focused on providing practical, pragmatic, hands-on strategies to help manage ADHD at the ground level of day to day life. It is about getting things done.

This book is about *how* to improve attention, concentration, and focusing ability. How to reduce procrastination. How to improve organization, efficiency, and productivity. How to succeed in school at any age and at any level. How to manage forgetfulness so that it does not cause problems. How to manage work, relationships, and daily life. These are the behavior skills that I wish someone had taught me during all my years in school, and in the early years of my professional career.

Now let's get to work.

CHAPTER 1

My Personal Journey
(Short Version)

THERE WAS NO NAME when I was growing up for what we now call ADHD. I was a bright enough student but half the time my mind was drifting, wandering down whatever interesting path just popped into my head. I was the forgetful child who, oh no, forgot to study for the spelling test again. And where did my mittens go? (Again!).

The teacher is talking about something or other, but I am completely lost in my drawing of the coolest concept car ever designed. My notebook is filled with abstract doodles that would make Picasso proud.

In high school things got more challenging because now I was on my own. I became very familiar with words like organization and procrastination. As in "you seriously need to work on organization," and "you're a real pro at procrastination!" But I was still a smart enough student and did enough to get by.

In college even I was beginning to think that, yeah, being a pro at procrastination maybe had a downside. Every single paper I ever wrote in college was written the night before it was due. Every – single – paper.

By junior year I had a routine down. I would do some of the readings, take some notes, then finally sit down at my desk around 8:00 PM the evening before the paper was due. I had my usual six-pack of Dr. Pepper and a box of No-Doz (caffeine pills), and then and only then did I start writing. With a major boost from the sugar, caffeine, and adrenaline, by 6:00 AM or so the next morning the paper was written (whew!). Then I spent the rest of the day walking around half asleep and exhausted.

Never again, I promised myself. No way! Until, of course, the next paper was due. Hello desk, Dr. Pepper, No-Doz. I could not for the life of me get myself to sit down and start writing until it was do-or-die, back against the wall, panic time.

This would drive me nuts, but I simply did not under-stand it. Worse, I felt powerless to change it.

Later, much later, I learned about biology and neuro-chemistry and things like "activation difficulty" that drive this type of behavior. At that time however the on-ly explanation I could give myself was that I was "lazy." Yep, that had to be it. I was simply lazy, there was noth-ing I could do about it, and that was that.

In graduate school I didn't get all the reading done in most of my classes, but I learned what I needed to know. It helped tremendously that I had a strong natural interest in the subject matter of psychology. That made grad school easier and more interesting than college. Somehow, through sheer obstinate determination, I made it all the way through a Ph.D. program in Clinical Psychology.

"Hey, That Sounds Like Me!"

My first job working in a clinic as a psychologist involved working with children who were considered to be academic underachievers. This was in 1985, only a few years after the publication of DSM-III, the latest version at that time of the Diagnostic and Statistical Manual for mental health professionals.

This DSM included a new-fangled diagnosis called Attention Deficit Disorder, which everyone soon called ADD for short ("ADHD" came later, in 1987). This was so new that it was never even discussed in my diagnostic classes in graduate school.

It became obvious in working with these children who were "performing below ability level" that many of them were kids with ADD. Can't stay focused while reading, or doing homework, or cleaning his or her room, or whatever else they're supposed to be working on. Take forever to get anything done, so one hour of homework stretches into two or three.

Many (not all) of these kids were fidgety, restless, easily bored, and highly impatient. They kept misplacing and losing their homework and other stuff. Or they did their homework, but forgot to turn it in. They talked too much and were disruptive in class. They lost their mittens (again!).

As I learned more about this ADD stuff and worked with these delightful but frustrated children, it slowly dawned on me: *"Hey, that sounds like me!"*

Many adults with ADHD will tell you that the "sounds like me" moment of clarity and understanding is often a transformational experience. It's as if a cloud of thick fog clears away, and things that previously made no sense start to finally make some sense. This is the first break-through: simple basic awareness. It makes possible all the coping skills, life management strategies, and other good stuff that comes later.

On A Mission

Don't let anyone ever tell you that people with ADHD cannot focus well. That is one of the most common mis-conceptions, but it's simply not true. People with ADHD can focus extremely well (we sometimes call it "hyperfo-cusing") on *things that interest them strongly.* It's all the other stuff, the routine and boring stuff, that they tend to struggle with.

This phenomenon of human behavior applies to every-one of course – we *all* focus better on things that interest us strongly – but it applies to people with ADHD to an extreme level. (Much more on that later).

I already had a strong interest in ADHD from working with my academic underachievers, but once I gained the "this is me" insight I was on a mission that will last the rest of my life. What had been a professional interest now also became a personal interest. Very personal.

I absorbed information from books and online resources. I discovered a new organization that called itself ChADD

(Children with ADD), and attended their national conferences starting with the 3rd annual conference. I became a sponge for knowledge. That, my friends, is called being focused.

Besides my interest in learning I also developed a passion for educating others about ADHD. In the mid-1990's the most common way to get internet access was through a paid service called America Online (AOL). I started a weekly, 90 minute online chat group on AOL called "Ask Dr. ADD." I used my real name, but "Ask Dr. ADD" was easier to remember and more catchy than "Ask Dr. Jaksa."

Imagine dozens of people in an online chat room, typing questions and comments, and me typing furiously to keep up. The discussion group lasted for four years until I became too busy and had to give it up. AOL never paid me a dime, but that did not matter. The opportunity to educate and share knowledge was deeply satisfying.

The one regret I had (and still have) is that at times I would get hundreds of emails in a day and did not have the time or the staff to answer most of them. So, to anyone who emailed "Ask Dr. ADD" back then and never received an answer – please accept this belated apology.

What about the Adults? The ADDA Mission

In 1998 I was asked to join the Board of Directors of a national nonprofit organization, Adults With ADD (ADDA). While ChADD was started and run primarily by parents and teachers with an interest in children with ADHD, ADDA was a group of adults with ADHD who were asking "hey, what about us!" This was at a time when many doctors were mistakenly still telling parents "don't worry, he (or she) will grow out of it."

While ChADD was getting funding in the millions of dollars, ADDA was a voice in the wilderness relying on volunteer work and struggling to keep an office afloat in Ohio. Its conferences were joyful tribal gatherings of adults with ADHD, but some lost money.

By 1999 the organization was deeply in debt and the Board was getting burnt out. The decision was made to terminate ADDA unless some brave (or foolish) soul with more passion than common sense volunteered to take over and be responsible for making the organization work.

Hey look, a challenge! Sure, I said, I'll be the new President. We'll pay off the debts. We'll recruit a new Board. Send all the boxes from the office in Ohio to me. We can't afford office space right now, but I have room in my garage in Chicago.

More than a challenge, this also became a mission. Adults with ADHD needed a voice to educate the public and advocate for them. Within six months ADDA put on a conference that earned a healthy profit and paid off the organization's debts. Within two years ADDA was on solid footing. It continues to be a thriving organization today, and a voice of education, support, and advocacy.

Getting ADDitude

In 1998 I was approached by a lovely lady named Ellen Kingsley with ideas for a new project. Ellen had been a network TV correspondent for NBC News, but now her primary focus was her young daughter with ADHD. She wanted to start a national magazine aimed at educating the general public about ADHD. Would I help with fund-raising and contributing articles to the magazine?

My agreement was immediate and enthusiastic. There was an obvious need for practical and useful information geared to a general public audience, in addition to the professional journals and newsletters. Beyond that Ellen's genuine caring and compassionate interest as a parent was compelling.

Ellen launched the project as the publisher of *ADDitude Magazine,* and it became an immediate success. The magazine still thrives today. It also reaches an even wider audience of millions of people through its website. It is my go-to location when people ask about finding useful and pragmatic information about ADHD.

We lost Ellen much too early when she lost her battle with cancer in 2007. Her legacy as an educator and advocate lives on after her.

The Mission Continues

It has been 35 years since my "aha!" moment of insight in 1985, which launched a life-long career of working with people of all ages with ADHD. I have had the privilege to work with people in almost any profession you can name, many of them exceptionally creative and productive people with outstanding success in their fields. Experience has taught me well about the universality of ADHD genetics and biology, and also about the practical day to day realities of living with ADHD.

As I continue my efforts to help individuals and families, and to educate individuals and the public, I also continue to learn more about this very complex bit of human biology. Writing this book is my effort to share the knowledge of 35 years of working with and learning from thousands of people with ADHD.

The mission continues.

CHAPTER 2

What Is ADHD?

LET US BEGIN WITH some basic concepts and facts about ADHD. These will be discussed in some detail in this chapter. Real life examples will be provided as we go along in the book.

Plainly stated, ADHD is a genetic part of human biology, found among people all over the world. It is most likely as old as the human race. It has some positive qualities associated with it, and also some negative qualities.

Some key points to keep in mind:

- ADHD is a brain *difference* – it is not a brain *disorder*. It is biology, not pathology. Pathology might be cured, but biology should be managed. Much more about this as we go along.

- ADHD is a *continuum* of behavior – it is not a *category* of behavior. Every single ADHD "symptom" is common ordinary behavior.

- ADHD is not something you "catch," and there is no "onset" at a certain point in life. This is consistent biology that is there from day one and lasts a lifetime.

- ADHD is not an "affliction" – but neither is it a "gift." It has both negative and positive qualities.

- ADHD is universal, found in different populations all around the world.

- ADHD is nothing new. It most likely has been around forever.

- ADHD has a very strong genetic component. It runs in families.

- ADHD is not a disease or an illness, therefore it cannot be "cured."

- People with ADHD who have a good understanding of their biology, and find strategies and resources that fit their particular needs, have unlimited opportunities for success and happiness in life. Just like everyone else.

Brain Difference vs Brain Disorder

The brains of people with ADHD are just as healthy as the brains of anyone else. They may be "wired" a little differently in certain ways, for example having lower levels of the neurotransmitter dopamine in the prefrontal cortex, or showing small differences in tissue volume in certain parts of the brain.

These differences are a matter of variation in brain chemistry and structure, and *not* a matter of brain disease or disorder. The ADHD brain is not "damaged" – and shame on those who would argue otherwise.

"Continuum" vs "Category" of Behavior

There is one essential factor about ADHD that must be properly understood, otherwise the person fails to "get" ADHD completely. *Every symptom of ADHD is normal, ordinary behavior, that in some people happens too frequently or too intensely.* That's it. That's all ADHD is.

What makes the behaviors "ADHD" is that they are at times excessive. Everyone is distracted occasionally -- but if you can't get through two paragraphs of reading without being distracted, then it becomes a problem. Everyone procrastinates occasionally -- but if procrastination becomes a way of life that makes you inefficient in school, at your job, or at home, then it becomes a problem.

Everyone gets impatient or restless occasionally -- but if you get so restless that you're constantly fidgeting or have to move, and get very uncomfortable sitting through a class or a meeting, then it can be a problem.

Many people intuitively understand this about ADHD "symptoms," which is why you sometimes hear statements such as "everybody has ADHD." Well, no, actually that statement is not true.

What makes it ADHD, as opposed to typical or "average" distractibility, procrastination, or fidgeting and restlessness, is that the frequency and/or intensity of the behavior is so high that it starts to cause problems for the person. The clinical term, which is required for a clinical diagnosis, is *impairment*.

The tricky thing about ADHD biology and impairment is that impairment can be highly situational. Some people struggle while they're in school, but have no problems after they complete their education. Some do great in certain (high interest) classes, but very poorly in other (low interest) classes. Some struggle in certain kinds of jobs, but excel in other jobs. "Impairment" varies widely over time and situations.

In short, ADHD is a *continuum* in a range of certain types of behaviors that we see in all people everywhere. Even among people with ADHD we see a wide range of behaviors from "mild" ADHD to "severe" ADHD.

What, on the other hand, makes behavior fit the definition of a *category*? These are behaviors that are fundamentally different from usual, normal behavior that is common to all people. Hallucinations and delusions that sometimes occur with schizophrenia and psychosis are one example. Suicidal behavior that can occur with severe clinical depression is another.

There is no "Onset" of ADHD

A mental illness such as schizophrenia usually emerges later in life, most commonly during adolescence or adulthood, when there are significant changes in brain chemistry. People are not born with schizophrenia. The same applies to clinical depression or bipolar disorder. We can usually point to an onset of symptoms at a certain age for certain people. Symptoms may come and go at different points in the person's life. There are periods of remission when symptoms go away, sometimes permanently. This is how illnesses work.

There is no such thing as adolescent or adult "onset" of ADHD. ADHD biology is there from birth and lasts for a lifetime. This is not something you "catch," it does not come and go, and it does not go away. There are no periods of remission with ADHD. This is *not* how illnesses work.

Very often people with ADHD do fine until they reach high school, for example, or college, or medical school, or a job promotion to a high level position. At that point they might struggle with the increased workload because their usual coping strategies are no longer efficient enough. They did not however suddenly "catch" ADHD – the ADHD was there all along. Their brain chemistry did not change and their brains did not suddenly develop a "disorder."

Neither "Scourge" Nor "Gift"

Over the years I have heard ADHD referred to as an affliction, a disease, a mental illness, a curse, a scourge, and other execrable terms that I've forgotten. These are unfair, inaccurate, and destructive labels to place on any person.

Sadly, much too often these are labels that a person with ADHD places on himself or herself. Even worse, these are labels that a person sometimes places on the behavior of a child that he or she is parenting, teaching, or treating. The negativity is misplaced and it is always destructive.

ADHD is biology that involves a variety of both negative and positive qualities. Illnesses and diseases are afflictions with no redeeming positive qualities. ADHD has nothing in common with that.

On the other extreme of the positive-negative spectrum are some well-intentioned folks who want to describe ADHD as a "gift." They would prefer to focus on the positive qualities of ADHD behavior (creativity, empathy, passion, energy, etc.) and minimize or ignore the problematic behaviors (excessive distractibility, procrastination, forgetfulness, inconsistent behavior, etc.).

While I understand the wish to counter the destructive negativity, I don't believe that either extreme in viewpoints is necessary or helpful. ADHD is biology. It is neither all bad nor all good.

ADHD Is Common Biology Found All Over the World

In my long career I have worked with people with ADHD who were born on every continent except Antarctica. This is not an exaggeration.

ADHD biology is the same all over the world. A person with ADHD from North America is no different from one in Asia. One from Africa is no different from one from Australia. One from South America is no different from one from Europe.

Individuals with ADHD vary widely in terms of frequency and intensity of specific behaviors, but the core spectrum of behaviors that we call ADHD is the same everywhere. They are part of the genetic code of the human race, and as best we know are found in approximately 5% of the world population.

ADHD Biology Is Nothing New

The name Attention Deficit Hyperactivity Disorder, usually shortened to ADHD, is a modern invention. It only became an official diagnosis with the publication of DSM-III-R in 1987. The biology of ADHD however has very likely been around forever.

Behavioral stereotypes of boys like "Fidgety Phil" and girls like "Chatty Cathy" go back centuries, if not millennia. No doubt some poor kid in ancient Babylon got chastised for misplacing his clay tablets – again!

ADHD behaviors were given labels that implied pathology only within the past one hundred years or so. In the United States in the 1940's and 1950's some children were diagnosed with MBD, which stood for Minimal Brain Damage. The purported evidence was that they showed "soft neurological signs" such as excessive distractibility and hyperactivity.

Evidently the term Minimal Brain Damage was deemed too harsh (and there was no evidence of any "brain damage"), so the MBD diagnosis was changed to Minimal Brain Disorder. This apparently was considered progress at the time.

ADHD has nothing to do with brain damage of course, and "brain disorder" is a matter entirely open to interpretation. Unfortunately that did not prevent untold thousands of children from being labeled with a horrific and stigmatizing diagnosis. The current medical model of ADHD, also unfortunately, has still not moved far beyond that.

ADHD Has a Very Strong Genetic Component

ADHD runs in families. The heritability of ADHD (.91) is very similar to the heritability of height (.90). In some families it runs very strongly, with many close relatives showing the behavior patterns. In some families it runs less frequently. Sometimes it skips a generation or two. In other words, ADHD biology behaves like most genetic phenomena behave in the human population.

ADHD Cannot Be "Cured" (But It Can Be Managed Well)

We cannot "cure" something that is not an illness. You cannot "cure" ADHD any more than you can "cure" your eye color. Instead we focus on helping individuals with ADHD to manage any behaviors associated with ADHD that might be causing problems for her or him at that point in time. The approach must be individualized and uniquely designed for each person. What works, what doesn't, and why, is addressed in detail in Chapter 3, "Multimodal Management of ADHD."

In my career I have worked with students of all ages, and with adults with ADHD engaged in a very wide variety of jobs and occupations. Teachers, lawyers, auto mechanics, sales people, artists, surgeons, accountants, managers, and business executives. They all share some common behavioral characteristics, to some degree, but of course each is a unique individual with unique interests, strengths, and weaknesses.

What every person with ADHD has in common is the ability to learn, to set goals, and to change behavior. ADHD biology is no road block to whatever career a person chooses, if she or he has the talent for it and puts in the effort necessary for success. No different from anyone else.

Ten Myths and Misconceptions about ADHD

■ *"ADHD is not real."*
  o One still sometimes hears this silly statement. Often the comment is made in order to criticize the person with ADHD. Sometimes it is made out of sheer ignorance. In either case it must be rejected as something not worth being taken seriously.

  o *"It's just an excuse for irresponsible and lazy behavior."* This comes from someone playing the blame game. Parents and teachers are often the victims of the blame game.

  o *"ADHD is an American invention."* Completely untrue. People with ADHD are found all around the world, in every race, culture, and region.

  o *"There is no physical test for ADHD, which shows it's not real."* Completely irrelevant. This is not a physical illness or disease.

  o *"Who says ADHD is real?"* Just for starters: The American Medical Association. The American Psychological Association. The U.S. Department of Education. The U.S. Department of Justice. Every credible professional organization in the world.

■ *"Everybody has ADHD."*
  o This is a common misconception among people who lack a basic understanding about ADHD.

o It is true that behaviors such as being distracted, disorganized, procrastinating, being forgetful, and so on, are behaviors that "everybody does."

o What takes these behaviors into the "ADHD range" is that they happen excessively – too frequently and/or too intensely. If these behaviors are causing significant problems for the person, that makes them "ADHD symptoms." And no, it is not true that *everybody* has significant problems related to these common behaviors.

■ *"People with ADHD can't pay attention."*
    o This is a widely held belief. The belief is only partially true, which can make it difficult to understand.

    o Attention is situation specific. This is true for everyone, with or without ADHD.

    o Everyone pays attention better when engaged in something that interests them strongly. The difference for people with ADHD is that typically they can pay attention well *only* when they are engaged in something that interests them strongly. Inconsistency and variability in performance is the essence of ADHD.

■ *"Children outgrow ADHD when they grow up."*
    o Once a commonly accepted misconception, this is thankfully rarely heard anymore. Children do not "outgrow" ADHD, with one partial exception...

    o Hyperactivity and impulsivity often get milder with age for some people. Some children who are hyperactive and impulsive are significantly less so as they get into their late teens and early 20's. For others the hyperactivity and impulsivity lasts throughout their adult years.

■ *"ADHD is a learning disability."*
   o Simply put, it is not, although they can co-occur. ADHD and learning disabilities are different things that involve different aspects of brain functioning.

   o Learning disabilities involve difficulty with processing information in specific areas. (e.g., reading, mathematics, written language, nonverbal).

   o Co-occurrence of ADHD and LD can be high. Some research indicates that 25% of people with ADHD also have a co-occurring learning disability.

■ *"If you do well in school (or work) you don't have ADHD."*
   o This one misconception in particular can drive adults with ADHD nuts. I have heard of many, many instances where people were told by health care professionals (who should know better) that "you're too high functioning to have ADHD." Excuse my language if this sounds harsh, but that is pure idiocy.

   o Many people with ADHD are very successful at what they do. The more pertinent question is, how hard do they have to work to overcome their high levels of distractibility, disorganization, procrastination, etc.? When a successful professional has to consistently put in a 70 hour work week to accomplish what her peers accomplish in 45 or 50 hours, that may realistically be viewed as an indicator of "impairment."

o Many bright people with ADHD do very well in school, through grade school, high school, college, even graduate programs. At some point some people hit a biological ceiling where their talents and hard work are no longer sufficient to maintain a high level of performance. That point may come in college, in law school, or after getting a promotion to a very demanding job. If any person is ever again told "you're in medical school, you can't have ADHD," please run don't walk and find a different provider.

■ *"If you don't respond to ADHD medications, you don't have ADHD."*

o This is sometimes a misconception held by lay people. It is a mistake that should *never* be made or practiced by any health care professional.

o Response to medication should *never* be used as a basis for either confirming or rejecting a diagnosis of ADHD.

o No medications work for everyone.

o Getting the dosage level right is just as important as getting the medication right.

o Medication management should also take into account any co-existing conditions, which can complicate response to ADHD medications.

■ *"ADHD medications work differently in children and adults."*

  o Simply put, no.

  o ADHD medications are not designed to work for children or for adults. Their efficacy is not dependent on age level.

■ *"There is nothing good about ADHD."*

  o This is sometimes a refrain heard from a few "experts" in the field. Somehow they manage to present this negative opinion as an "evidence based" fact, when there is absolutely no "evidence" to back it up. Bizarrely, they seem to take satisfaction in expressing this negative view.

  o Based on my experience working with thousands of people with ADHD, and also working with dozens of experts in the field, I am strongly in the "yes" column when it comes to viewing some aspects of ADHD biology as beneficial, in many ways, for many people.

  o The creative business entrepreneurs, the performers and entertainers, the highly dedicated teachers, nurses, and doctors, and all the other passionate and driven people with ADHD in all walks of life know who they are. ADHD does not make them *who* they are (people are much more complicated than that), but many will tell you that ADHD makes them better at what they do. That fits most definitions of "benefits."

■ *"People with ADHD are not successful in life."*

  o Another bit of negative nonsense from people with limited understanding or distorted perceptions. Millions of very successful people with ADHD know this is a lie.

CHAPTER 3

Multimodal
Management of ADHD

RESEARCH AND EXPERIENCE SHOW with no doubt whatsoever that the most effective way to manage ADHD is with a combination of biological and behavioral approaches. In the professional literature this is referred to as a multi-modal approach. Basically it means using a variety of techniques and resources, which makes perfect sense when dealing with a biological phenomenon that impacts behavior in many ways in many areas of life.

This chapter will discuss a number of biological interventions, behavioral strategies, healthy lifestyle factors, and diet and nutrition factors. Nothing works for everyone, however each of these strategies can provide some benefits for some individuals. The most productive approach is to find what strategies work best for you, use it, and stick with it.

Biological and Behavioral Strategies

The two interventions that make the biggest impact in terms of brain chemistry is medication (for people who choose to take medication) and aerobic exercise. Both can provide very significant benefits for many individuals with ADHD. Medication management will be covered separately in Chapter 4 ("Medication Management and ADHD"), because it is a very complicated subject and requires a more detailed discussion.

Behavioral management of ADHD is just as important as biological interventions, and in some cases even more so. ADHD biology affects performance across a wide range of behaviors including organization, time management, planning and prioritizing, managing emotionality and affect, and forgetfulness.

Even in cases where individuals get benefits from medication and exercise, many still need to work on developing strategies and routines that allow them to work efficiently and productively. It is eminently true that "pills don't teach skills."

Healthy lifestyle behaviors are important for overall health and wellbeing, but are also essential for managing ADHD well. In particular maintaining a regular sleep cycle, maintaining a healthy and balanced schedule, and managing stress reasonably well are extremely important. It should come as no surprise that many people with ADHD tend to be very inconsistent in all three of those areas.

There are no magic foods for ADHD. That said however, good nutrition and healthy eating habits are a very important part of managing ADHD well. A balanced diet is necessary to prevent nutritional deficiencies, which are bad for overall health and also cause problems in many areas of cognitive functioning. Maintaining a healthy blood sugar level, by eating regular meals and healthy snacks, has a very big impact on attention, concentration, activation, mood, and memory functioning.

Cardiorespiratory (Aerobic) Exercise

The benefit from stimulant medications is primarily that they increase levels of dopamine. The benefits from regular aerobic exercise is that they increase levels of *all* monoamine neurotransmitters including dopamine, serotonin, and norepinephrine. The research on this is extensive and incontrovertible. Higher levels of neurotransmitters elevate mood, improve attention and focusing ability, and reduce anxiety and feelings of stress.

In terms of brain benefits, working out aerobically is like taking a bit of Adderall, a bit of Prozac, and a bit of Valium – without actually taking the medications. If you happen to be taking one or more of those medications, the aerobic workouts give you benefits in addition to any benefits you might be getting from the medication. All without any unpleasant side effects or prescription costs. What's not to like?

An optimally effective workout program needs to be personalized to fit your needs, interests, and temperament. In designing your workout program consider the following:

- It should fit your *health level*. Before starting a workout program discuss it with your medical doctor.

- It should fit your *fitness level*. If you don't work out hard enough you will not benefit as much. If you work out too intensely you risk getting injured, or simply get to hate the workouts and give up on them.

- To be consistent your workout needs some structure. For most people that means a workout schedule. No way around that – otherwise settle for being inconsistent.

- Schedule different types of activities that you enjoy to give your workout program *variety*. (Repetition gets boring for the ADHD brain much faster than for most people). Run one or two days a week, swim one or two days, go for a bike ride, play basketball, take a workout class or two.

- Work with a personal trainer to design your personalized workout. It should be balanced for frequency (how often you work out) and for intensity (how long and how hard you work out), both taking into account your health and fitness levels.

- Get a workout buddy, or work with a personal trainer, to help you maintain the workout program over time. Starting a workout program can be interesting, but the real hard work is *sticking with it*.

Anyone who has followed a workout program is familiar with the "runner's high" that you feel immediately after you finish a workout. It is a wonderful feeling of very positive mood, relaxation, and energy. That feeling is caused by a rush of endorphins. Unfortunately it typically only lasts for 60 to 90 minutes.

The benefits of aerobic exercise last 24 hours a day, seven days a week – more focused, better mood, physically calmer and less hyper, more patient, less impulsive, less avoidance behavior and procrastination. The elevated levels of dopamine, serotonin, and norepinephrine stay elevated long-term for as long as you maintain the workout schedule.

Focus like an Olympian (Here's to you, Mr. Phelps)

Many years ago I read about the life of Michael Phelps, the Olympic swimmer who has won 23 gold medals and is considered to be the greatest swimmer in history. Over the years I have told his story to hundreds of people, and it never fails to inspire.

The very short version is this. Michael was one of those very hyperactive children who was diagnosed with ADHD at a young age. He was prescribed a stimulant medication that toned down the hyperactivity but only up to a point. Because he was so active his mother signed him up for swimming classes.

What was fascinating for me, from a human interest and also an ADHD biology perspective, was that the intense swimming workouts did as much or more for him than his medication.

Very few if any of us will be working out as actively as Mr. Phelps did during his active swimming career, but the point still remains. Regular aerobic exercise provides very substantial benefits for people who wish to manage their ADHD well.

Managing Time

The *how* of various behavior strategies and organization skills will be covered in detail in many of the remaining chapters in this book. This section will briefly discuss the *why* – why are behavior strategies so important, and sadly why are they so often overlooked and neglected.

For a variety of reasons time management skills do not come naturally for many people with ADHD. As with most things it starts with biology. Individuals with ADHD tend to live in the moment, respond to the immediate, then respond to the next interesting thing. (Oops, just got off task – again.)

This living in the moment is a biological imperative. People do not look ahead, and thus do not plan ahead. This is not a matter of not being *able* to plan – many people with ADHD are surprisingly good at planning – but rather the problem is that people simply don't take the time or make the effort to *do* the planning. Sometimes we're "too busy" to plan (a big mistake), but more likely we simply don't think about it.

Lack of planning often leads to jumping from one thing to another -- either getting distracted by what is interesting in the moment, or putting out the fires from things that should have been done but never did get done. Life on a daily basis can turn into a series of putting out fires. Some of these may be little fires, but some unfortunately will be damaging and costly fires.

The only solution to a life of not bothering to manage time, and thus inadvertently inviting chaos, is to develop a system for time management and to use it judiciously. The goal is not to become efficient at putting out fires, but rather to *prevent* fires from starting in the first place. Chapter 9 ("Improve Time Management") will explore strategies for time management and fire prevention.

Managing Things

The other major form of organization, besides managing time, is managing things. These are the things of ordinary life that we work with, play with, and live with. The things that, for many people with ADHD, ends up in a pile of stuff somewhere or other. Or possibly under the couch. And where did my phone charger go?

Imagine a 9 year old boy coming home from school (or a 6 year old, or 12 year old). The coat goes flying in one direction. The backpack gets discarded somewhere, it does not matter where. If he stopped to think about it, he knows very well there is a coat hook by the door on which to hang up his coat ("how many times do I have to remind you, Jason?"), but still the coat ends up on the couch or on the floor.

It's not that Jason is trying to be inconsiderate or rebellious. Not at all, and he would be surprised to be called those things. He's actually a pretty nice kid who wants to please his parents. What happens in that moment when Jason walks in the door is that his mind is completely somewhere else – getting a snack from the kitchen, checking Facebook, resuming his video game, any one of a dozen other things.

The coat does not get hung on the coat hook because in that moment neither the coat nor the coat hook, nor the constant reminders from Mom and Dad, exist in Jason's mind. He is completely focused on that one thing on his mind and nothing else. We all do this from time to time, of course. For people with ADHD it happens all the time and becomes a way of life. It can also drive people like Jason's Mom and Dad crazy (even if one or both also have ADHD).

Human nature dictates that behavior which is repeated many times, over an extended period of time, becomes ingrained as strong habits. In time Jason grows up, and perhaps becomes a teacher, an accountant, or a salesman. Unless he works on developing and using some organizational systems, the ways that he managed his coat and backpack will translate to the ways he manages his files, his lesson plans, or his work materials and equipment. Things end up in piles, and Jason wastes a great deal of time searching for things that are somewhere or other.

Clutter Prevention

Organizing stuff does not come naturally for most people with ADHD. Many people don't have the patience for it. Organizing is, well, boring. Many people reach a point of frustration where the clutter becomes painful, then attack the mess with a passion. Ah, my home is organized at last! All too often, within a week or two, the old clutter is back again because the old habits are still in place.

The solution for being disorganized is not clutter clean-up, but rather *clutter prevention*. It takes developing a system that feels right for that person, and provides sufficient structure for that person's needs. Chapter 8 ("De-clutter Your Environment") examines strategies for managing one's stuff and surroundings.

Healthy Lifestyle Behaviors

Healthy lifestyle behaviors are important for overall health and wellbeing. They are also essential for managing ADHD well. At the top of the list is getting into a regular sleep cycle and making sure that you're getting enough restful sleep, maintaining a balanced schedule, and managing stress well.

Do NOT Be Sleep Deprived

Sleep deprivation makes ADHD biology worse. It is bad for mental alertness and focusing ability, bad for activation (getting started), bad for memory functioning and forgetfulness, bad for impulsivity and emotional overreaction.

There is no way around it – if you are a person with ADHD and you're not getting enough healthy sleep, you will have more difficulty with managing some of the negative ADHD behaviors. Unfortunately people who struggle with inconsistency also struggle to maintain a consistent sleep routine and schedule.

Many children with ADHD hate bedtime, the reason most often being that "it's boring." They simply want to keep doing whatever they were doing. Adolescents with ADHD can be very erratic in getting involved in one activity or another and staying up very late. College students with ADHD are notorious for inconsistent sleep habits, which can lead to problems with chronic sleep deprivation.

Many adults with ADHD, who "should know better" and actually *do* know better, still struggle with maintaining a regular sleep schedule. Sometimes it's a matter of being so involved in what they're doing that they lose track of time. Sometimes it's a matter of "one more thing" syndrome. Let me finish washing the dishes first, or check my email first, or finish this chapter in the book, or check whatever Jennifer or Jeff posted on social media. Most commonly however it's a simple matter of "don't feel like it."

Sleep habits are very strong habits that evolve over many years. Changing them can be a difficult and frustrating process. If sleep deprivation becomes part of a person's lifestyle however, it is imperative to work on changing them.

The price you pay for sleep deprivation is simply too high – not only in terms of poor attention and negative mood, but in terms of health problems such as higher risks for obesity, hypertension, heart disease, and heart attacks.

I have heard the excuse that "I'm taking medication for ADHD so I don't need much sleep." That is simply not true. Even if you are taking medication, and even if the medication is providing benefits for you, the negative effects of sleep deprivation will decrease the effectiveness of the medication. You are always working against yourself by neglecting sleep.

Consistency requires structure. The only way to get into and maintain a consistent sleep schedule is to get into a bedtime routine, including some regular bedtime that you can live with.

Establish a STOP time. This is the trigger that says STOP – my day is done. Stop whatever you are doing. Put things away. Turn off electronics. Don't allow yourself to get into "one more thing" mode.

When You Can't Fall Asleep

Some people are sleep deprived because they have problems falling asleep or staying asleep. For many people, particularly at the high end of the hyperactivity scale, it's a matter of "my brain just won't shut down." Anxiety can also exacerbate that problem.

Using electronic devices such as smart phones and computers close to bedtime can keep the brain overstimulated and make it more difficult to fall asleep. It is generally a good idea to shut down "blue screen" electronics at least one hour before bedtime.

If sleep disorders are a factor, they need to be identified and treated. Insomnia is common, but also treatable. Sleep apnea is a serious medical condition that not only prevents restful sleep but can also be life threatening. If sleep apnea is suspected it should be evaluated via a sleep study and treated. Restless leg syndrome, which affects one in twenty adults, can cause chronic sleep problems and should be evaluated and treated.

Sleep Aids

Some herbal and organic sleep enhancers, such as chamomile tea and valerian root tea, can make it easier to fall asleep. Chamomile is a natural tranquilizer that has been used as a herbal medicine for centuries.

Melatonin is a hormone released by the Pineal gland to help induce sleep and regulate sleepiness and wakefulness. Its release is stimulated by darkness and suppressed by light. Taking a melatonin supplement can be useful for treating insomnia and jet lag.

Even short periods of meditation, before bedtime or while in bed, can be helpful in quieting the mind and falling asleep. A simple self-hypnosis technique, such as counting sheep jumping over a fence, can do the same.

Maintain a Healthy Sleep Cycle

Many people wonder, "how much sleep *should* I be getting?" The general answer is that most people need between seven and nine hours of sleep per night. The more specific answer is "listen to what your body tells you." Are you waking up feeling reasonably rested and awake? Is your energy level and level of alertness reasonably high and consistent throughout the day? If not, see if getting more sleep makes a difference.

When establishing a healthy sleep routine consider the following strategies:

- Maintain a regular sleep schedule with a firm bedtime
- Follow a bedtime ritual (brush teeth, put on pj's, etc.)
- Keep your bedroom dark
- Keep the room temperature on the low side
- Turn off electronics at least one hour before bedtime
- Avoid caffeine after early afternoon
- Invest in a good mattress and pillow

■ Do some light meditation while in bed

Food, Nutrition, and Blood Sugar Level

Although there are no magic foods for ADHD, it is very important to eat healthy and avoid nutritional deficiencies. What is equally as important is to eat regularly and maintain a healthy blood sugar level. Hypoglycemia, very low blood sugar level, caused by skipping breakfast or lunch for example, hurts attention, activation, mood management, and memory functioning.

When it comes to nutrition what works for the ADHD brain is no different than what works for everyone else. The essential fatty acids (Omega-3, EPA, DHA) found in fish oils, flaxseed and canola oil, soybeans, and walnuts, provide the same important benefits for everyone. They help to promote cell myelination, enhance neurotransmitter activity, and promote a healthy brain and nervous system.

A diet that includes healthy proteins (lean meats and poultry, eggs, nuts and seeds, legumes) and healthy carbohydrates (whole grains, fiber-rich fruits and vegetables, low-fat dairy, beans and legumes) are important for overall health and also for brain health and brain functioning.

Why Bad Nutrition is Very Bad News

Poor diets that are high in processed foods are associated with nutritional deficiencies in essential vitamins and minerals. *Diets high in processed sugars and carbs actually deplete the body of vitamins and essential minerals.*

Deficiencies in Vitamin D and Omega 3 are associated with depression, anxiety, and poor concentration. Deficiencies in magnesium are associated with mood dysregulation. Deficiencies in Vitamin B12 are associated with fatigue, memory problems, depression, and anxiety. These are only a few examples.

Let's be clear, ADHD is a matter of genetics and biology. It is not caused by nutritional deficiencies. On the other hand good nutrition helps to manage the biology of ADHD much better. Poor nutrition makes it more difficult, because it exacerbates problems with attention, memory, and mood regulation. The occasional pizza, donut, and diet soda is not going to ruin your life. A diet that includes them on a regular basis is asking for problems.

The Role of Supplements

Nutritional supplements are *not* a substitute for a healthy diet. Some supplements, however, can provide some benefits. Taking a quality multi-vitamin can help prevent deficiencies in vitamins and minerals. Ginseng helps regulate blood sugar levels, improves digestion, and helps to manage stress.

The vitamin shelves at your local pharmacy are full of products that list ADHD among the list of conditions that particular product is meant to help. Be clear that manufacturers of vitamins and other supplements are free to make any such claims without offering any proof whatsoever that those products provide those benefits. Medications are highly regulated. Nutritional supplements are not.

CHAPTER 4

Medication Management and ADHD

HAVING ADHD DOES NOT mean that a person *must* take medication, or even that he or she *should* take medication. The decision about using medication should always be a matter of personal choice. It should only be made after a careful and thorough consultation between the individual (or a parent or guardian) and their medical professional. Period. End of story.

Unfortunately following this basic and sound principle is not always what actually happens in the real world of health care. Many (not all) medical professionals routinely decide that a diagnosis of ADHD is followed by writing a prescription. Many adults with ADHD, or parents of children with ADHD, also accept that as routine and normal.

This is a predictable result of accepting the medical model, the "mental illness" or "brain disorder" model, of ADHD. This is, after all, what we typically do with illnesses and disorders – we medicate them.

What this process sometimes leads to is a lot of people, including many young children, being routinely (sometimes too routinely) put on medication when they might do okay with managing ADHD without medication. Based on statistics from the CDC (Centers For Disease Control and Prevention) upwards of 11% of American children are taking ADHD medications There are reports of some school districts where upwards of 40% of students are taking ADHD medications. It is difficult to see how this reflects sound clinical practice.

Informed Choices and Medical Need

ADHD is not an illness. This is not like having epilepsy, diabetes, hypertension, or schizophrenia. If you have a seizure disorder that requires medication, for example, if you don't take anti-seizure medication you face a higher risk for having seizures that can result in brain damage or death. In this situation medication is a god-send, and *not* taking medication would be a foolish and reckless decision.

If you have ADHD, if you don't take ADHD medication you simply continue with your baseline behavior in terms of distractibility, physical restlessness (if you're hyperactive), activation difficulty, and so on. You miss out on potential benefits that medication might provide for you in helping manage your ADHD biology easier. For some people this can be a problem. For others, not necessarily.

Some people, particularly those at the high end of the ADHD biology spectrum, find their baseline behavior to be difficult to manage at certain points in their lives. At those times they may find that the right medication provides very substantial benefits for them. Making an informed decision to take medication at those times, in consultation with their medical professional, is the most constructive and helpful decision.

ADHD Medications Work the Same for Everyone (ADHD or Not)

It is an under-appreciated fact that stimulant medications, commonly prescribed for ADHD, work the same and provide the same benefits for *all* people – whether or not they have ADHD. The truck driver *without* ADHD driving from Chicago to Seattle gets the same benefits in staying focused and alert as does the attorney *with* ADHD who needs to carefully review a 50 page legal document. The college student *without* ADHD who takes a stimulant (often obtained illegally) to help him cram for an exam gets the same benefits as the high school student *with* ADHD who needs to focus well in order to complete her term paper.

Same exact benefits of improved alertness and sustained concentration. The only difference is that in most cases the benefits for people with ADHD are even stronger when compared to people without ADHD.

In all of the above situations the medication is used as a tool in order to help a person complete a task. No one would claim that the truck driver or the college student had a "brain disorder" because they were helped with staying focused by taking a stimulant medication. No one should make that claim for the lawyer or the high school student either.

The ADHD Management Toolbox

Stimulants and other ADHD medications are best regarded as a tool that can be helpful for some people, to some degree, in some situations. They are used as tools of choice based on medical need.

No medications work for everyone, nor work equally well for everyone. ADHD medications provide strong benefits for some people, moderate to mild benefits for others, and little to no benefits for some. When they work well it can make it easier to get things done – but it's still up to the person to get them done.

Medication is one potential tool in the ADHD management toolbox. That box should also include behavior skills training, aerobic exercise, healthy nutrition, and healthy lifestyle behaviors including getting enough sleep, managing stress, and maintaining a balanced lifestyle.

When making a decision of whether or not to take ADHD medications, here are some questions and issues to consider and discuss with your medical professional:

- What are the potential benefits of ADHD medications for me?
- Do I want or need these benefits?
- What are the potential side effects?
- Which medications should I try?
- What about caffeine?
- What if I'm already taking other medications?
- How long do I need to take ADHD medication?

What Are the Benefits of ADHD Medications?

The question of medication benefits should always be a "for me" question. What can the medication do *for me*?

The ADHD medications that are most effective for most people, and are most commonly prescribed, are the stimulant class of medications. Stimulants essentially "wake up" the brain and promote higher levels of alertness, which helps the brain be more efficient in regulating cognitive functions, emotional functions, and motor behavior. Sometimes those behaviors are placed under a label of "executive functions" – but they are simply common, ordinary, self-regulating behaviors that all humans engage in.

The potential benefits to consider from ADHD medications include:

- *Improve attention and focusing ability.* Focus better and focus longer. This is the primary benefit many if not most people seek from ADHD medication. An effective medication reduces distractibility, which simply makes it easier to focus on what you're supposed to be focusing on at the moment.

- *Improve activation.* Makes it easier to get going and get started on things. Perhaps you don't need to fight yourself as hard to start work on whatever task you have been procrastinating about.

- *Tone down hyperactivity.* For those individuals with ADHD for whom hyperactivity and physical restlessness is a problem, medication could tone down the hyperactivity and fidgeting. In real life situations perhaps you sit through a class or meeting easier, or watch a movie without needing to get up and move around.

- *Reduce impulsivity.* Medication could tone down impulsivity and improve impulse control, for those who are too impulsive. In real life perhaps you don't jump in when a person is speaking to you and interrupt mid-sentence.

- *Modulate affect and emotionality.* Biologically most people with ADHD are simply more emotional than most people. They might feel strongly and react intensely, which makes some people more prone to over-react. In real life the benefits might be that you don't get irritated or frustrated as easily, or don't react as quickly or intensely when upset.

The question of "how do I know if the medicine is working" is much easier to answer if you know what benefits to expect. Discuss this with your medical professional, learn how to monitor yourself well, and provide the medical professional with feedback in order to make adjustments as necessary.

Do I Want or Need These Benefits?

That should be the first question asked when it comes to using *any* medication. When it comes to treating something like diabetes or seizure disorder, the question is clearly and obviously "yes." When it comes to taking medication to help manage ADHD, the answer is more complicated and ultimately comes down to a personal choice that also takes into account medical advice. Please discuss the matter with your doctor or other medical professional.

One factor to consider is that individuals with ADHD vary widely in terms of how their ADHD biology impacts behavior, in what areas, and to what degree. Generally speaking the greater the intensity and impact of ADHD biology, the greater the frequency and "severity" of ADHD symptoms, the more likely that the individual would need or benefit from ADHD medications.

Another factor to consider are the current circumstances in the person's life. Some people choose to take ADHD medications while they are in school. Some take it when faced with a difficult job, a job promotion, or other life circumstances. Some people take medication long term, because they find it helpful and worthwhile in managing their ADHD biology.

Medication is a tool. When does the tool fit the situation?

What Are The Potential Side Effects?

As with any medication, this is a question that should be discussed with your medical professional. Every medication has side effects. Simple aspirin, if used too much, can cause internal bleeding and send you to the hospital.

As a class of medication the stimulant medications are generally considered to be much "cleaner" in terms of side effects compared to many other medications, for example the SSRI anti-depressants.

Some of the common side-effects associated with stimulant medications include the following:

- *Appetite suppression.* Stimulant medications can decrease appetite. For some people this side effect is very strong, for others very mild. Some decades ago these medications were prescribed in large doses as "diet pills," which unfortunately led to abuse and gave stimulant medications a bad name.

- *Weight loss.* This may or may not be considered a problem. Many adults with ADHD are actually happy to lose a few pounds. On the other hand, weight loss can be a significant problem particularly for children who are on the thin side and have difficulty putting on weight. Some of these children benefit from taking a "drug holiday" to allow them to eat more and gain weight.

- *Sleep interference.* Stimulants wake up the brain. If the medication is still in your blood system at bedtime it may cause problems getting to sleep. Approximately 30% or more of people taking stimulant medication report some problems with insomnia. This side effect can usually be managed based on adjusting timing of when the medication is taken, and sometimes adjusting dosage.

- *Hypertension.* Stimulants increase blood pressure. For many people the increase is very mild and not a problem. If the person has high blood pressure, medical professionals will often either monitor it closely or else not prescribe a stimulant at all.

- *Anxiety and tension.* For some people stimulants will increase anxiety, irritability, and muscle tension (e.g., clenched jaw). For individuals with co-existing anxiety disorders they may exacerbate symptoms of anxiety.

- *"Flat" affect.* Some people report a "flattening" or dulling of affect or feelings. Some report that this feels like a "loss of creativity." Sometimes this may be due to the person not tolerating the medication well, or the dosage level being too high.

- *Stomachaches.* This is sometimes a problem when a person begins a new medication. It often goes away as the person adjusts to the medication.

- *Headaches.* Also sometimes a problem when the person first starts taking the medication.

- *Trigger bipolar disorder symptoms.* Stimulant medications can trigger symptoms of bipolar disorder for people who either currently have bipolar or are at risk for developing bipolar. If there is a personal history or family history of bipolar disorder, many medical professionals are very cautious or simply decline to prescribe a stimulant medication.

- *Trigger tic disorder symptoms.* Stimulant medications can trigger vocal tics or muscle tics for people with tic disorders.

Which Medications Should I Use?

This is entirely a decision to be made between your medical professional and you. As noted previously, the most commonly prescribed ADHD medications are the stimulant class of medications. All stimulants work basically the same and provide similar benefits.

Stimulant medications increase levels of the neurotransmitter dopamine by blocking neuronal reuptake and increasing the levels of available dopamine in the brain. Essentially stimulants operate as Selective Dopamine Reuptake Inhibitors, similar to the way that Selective Serotonin Reuptake Inhibitors (SSRI) medications work for treating depression.

Amphetamine-based stimulants both block reuptake and also somewhat increase production of dopamine. Methylphenidate-based stimulants appear to be better tolerated by some people, with reduced risks of side effects. Approximately 15% of people with ADHD tend to respond better to one or the other major class of stimulants, amphetamine or methylphenidate. It is not possible to predict ahead of time who would respond best to what.

Some medical professionals have a preference or a comfort level for working with certain medications. If you are comfortable with the information and medical advice given to you, it is best to follow that advice. (And if not, why are you working with this particular provider?).

Getting Medication Choices and Dosage Levels Right

What many ADHD experts in the medical field recommend is to start with one type of stimulant medication. Start with a low dose and gradually titrate dosage levels higher until you reach optimal benefits without experiencing unpleasant side effects. If you are happy with the results, stick with it.

If you are not quite satisfied with the benefits from the first stimulant medication, try a different type of stimulant. The same procedure is followed in terms of trying different dosage levels to find optimal benefits and avoid side effects.

If you are not satisfied with the benefits from the stimulant medications, the experts recommend, try a non-stimulant ADHD medication. While stimulants have been shown to work best for most people, they do not work for everyone and do not work equally well for everyone. For some people the non-stimulant medications work as well or better.

Bottom line – what works for you is what works for you. If you take medication, do it right. Getting the choice of medication right, and getting the dosage level right, are both very important factors. Work with your medical professional on finding what is most effective for you.

What About Caffeine?

Caffeine is a mild stimulant. Why do hundreds of millions of people around the world start their day with their morning cup of coffee? To wake up their brains. To focus better. To get going easier. To help them relax.

That said, caffeine is *not* an ADHD medication and should never be used as such. Unfortunately many adults with ADHD self-medicate with large amounts of caffeine (think pots of coffee, not cups).

The effects/benefits of caffeine are weak compared to stimulant medications. Worse, consuming caffeine in large amounts is not good for your general health. It is addictive. It could potentially trigger a heart arrhythmia and give you a heart attack.

Drinking caffeine beverages in moderation is fine, unless there are underlying health reasons not to. Self-medicating with large amounts of caffeine is always a bad idea.

What If I Am Already Taking Other Medications?

It is not at all uncommon for people taking ADHD medication to use it in combination with one or more other medications, particularly if they are dealing with co-existing conditions such as anxiety or depression.

How Long Do I Need To Take ADHD Medications?

Short answer, for as long as you think you need the benefits the medication provides. Some people take medication for ADHD management for months, some for years, some for decades. There is no one fits all strategy. As with taking any medication, discuss any planned changes with your medical professional beforehand.

CHAPTER 5

Pay Attention!

Strategies to Improve Concentration and Focusing Ability

MOST PEOPLE ASSOCIATE ADHD with difficulty paying attention. We know now that ADHD biology is much more complicated than that, however there is no denying that excessive distractibility is a problem for almost every person with ADHD. The more distracted a person is the more it slows down performance in school, at work, or simply doing things around the house. Being distracted too much, too often, can hurt communication and even impact relationships.

ADHD level distractibility is a notch (or two, or three) above "normal" distractibility that most people experience on a daily basis. It is important to understand that this high level of distractibility is pure biology. The problem is *not* that the person doesn't want to pay attention, or is making no effort to pay attention -- although the behavior might look that way at times. The problem rather is that even when the person is trying very hard to stay focused, his or her mind will wander and drift (internal distractibility), or get distracted by a noise or some commotion happening around them (external distractibility). All people do this occasionally. With ADHD it happens a lot.

Improving attention and focusing ability, so that people can focus well when they most *need* to focus, is an essential and critical part of managing ADHD. A combination of biological and behavioral strategies is most effective.

Get the Biology Right (Medication, Exercise, Sleep, Nutrition)

The most amazing attention-improving behavior strategies in the world will only provide limited benefits if you are not taking care of your ADHD at the physical and biological level. Chapter 3, "Multimodal Management of ADHD," discusses in detail the benefits from exercise, sleep, and nutrition.

- If you're taking medication, get the medication right so that you are getting maximum benefits from it (see Chapter 4, "Medication Management and ADHD"). Indeed the single most important benefit from ADHD medications, for most people, is to improve attention and focusing ability.

- Other than medication, what will provide the most benefits in improving attention and concentration at the biological level is a program of regular aerobic exercise.

- Sleep deprivation does terrible things for attention and focusing ability. Get into a regular and healthy sleep schedule, and stick with it.

- Low blood sugar levels, for example caused by skipping meals, does terrible things for attention and focusing ability. Eating healthy and eating regularly both have a big impact on attention and concentration.

Reduce or Eliminate Distractions

The world around us is full of distractions. Modern life in a technology rich environment makes it worse. For a person with ADHD, dealing with the external distractions of modern life on top of dealing with the internal distractions of a wandering mind, the result can be a chronic feeling of eternal distractibility.

The first step in reducing distractions is to manage your environment as effectively as you can. For many adults it helps to set up a "home office" at home, a dedicated work space where you go when you need to focus well and get work done (paying bills, working on taxes, writing papers or reports, etc.). This is where you keep your important materials that you need to work with, all in one place and organized.

Now, make this a toy-free and distraction-free zone. One of those distractions that need to be eliminated, as drastic as this may sound, could very well be your smart phone. You must be ruthless in eliminating whatever is likely to get you off task when you need to be productive. Smart phones and internet access on any device are terribly distracting.

The same principles apply to setting up a study space for school age children. Besides having regular study times, many children with ADHD benefit from having a dedicated study space. Again, try to eliminate distractions from this study space as well as you can. Internet access should be limited to only what is necessary to complete the assignment being worked on.

Reducing distractions at work offers less control, but can still be done. If you work at a desk organize your work space so that only the materials needed for the task at hand are in front of you. Put your smart phone away until you have a lunch break or other scheduled break. Limit internet access to the current task being worked on. No social media, news sites, sports sites, entertainment sites, etc., until lunch break.

If you work in a noisy part of the office, ask to be moved to a less noisy section if that is an option (this can usually be handled as a productivity issue without even mentioning ADHD). One strategy many teachers use to help children pay attention better is simply to have the child sit in the front of the class. The general goal is the same – improve attention by reducing distractions.

Get the Background Noise Right

Some people with ADHD focus best in a very quiet room. Any noise or other activity makes it difficult to get anything done. Some people with ADHD focus better in a busy coffee shop. A room that is completely quiet drives them nuts and makes it impossible to focus. Different strokes for different folks.

I have mediated many disagreements between children or adolescents with ADHD and their well-meaning parents over the question of playing music in the background while they are doing homework. Parents usually insist on complete quiet during study times.

It seemed counter-intuitive to the parents that the child could focus better on the schoolwork with music in the background, but in many cases those kids were right. They actually focused better and worked better with music playing in the background. Whatever works best for a person is what works for that particular person.

Be an Active Listener and Participant

Distractibility thrives on passive behavior. When you are kind of "just there," going through the motions but not really engaged in what is going on, your mind will wander all over the place. Whether in a one to one conversation or a group discussion, the best way to focus and remain focused is to be an active participant.

In a one-to-one conversation make eye contact with the person and maintain comfortable, intermittent eye contact throughout the conversation. This helps with making a connection and also with maintaining focus. Eye contact is basic to good interpersonal communication.

In a group situation such as a meeting, take very brief and concise notes to keep up with the content and flow of the conversation. Only write key words or phrases, not sentences or paragraphs. Jot down a key word or two to remind yourself of what you want to say when it is appropriate for you to speak. The more active and participatory your role in the discussion, the easier it becomes to focus and stay focused.

Be an Active Learner

When reading, take very brief notes so the information is summarized in outline form. Highlight reading material very sparingly – only key terms, names, or phrases. You want to be able to go back and skim over the material very quickly, but also the process of very selective high-lighting forces you to focus better while you are reading.

In a classroom be an active listener and an active learner. Take brief and concise notes. Engage the instructor and other students if class discussion is allowed. The worst strategy, in terms of maintaining attention and focus, is to sit there passively and waiting for the class to end.

Take Breaks

Healthy breaks, like healthy snacks, can be very good for you. They should be indulged in when appropriate, joyfully, thankfully, and with zero guilt tripping. We'll talk about what makes a "healthy" break in a moment.

A basic truth of ADHD biology is that the more distractible a person is, the more quickly she or he is likely to become mentally fatigued. This is because the higher level of distractibility, the more effort it takes to focus and stay focused. Even very capable, very bright people with ADHD will become mentally fatigued faster than most people. This is unrelated to intelligence, motivation, or how responsible the person is. It is simply a matter of how hard the person has to work at staying focused.

It is essential for individuals with ADHD to get good at monitoring themselves and become very aware of when the mental fatigue kicks in. That is the point to take a healthy break, because to persist doggedly with the task at hand is neither productive nor healthy. You keep working but little or nothing gets done. That is no doubt working hard – but perhaps not working very smart.

A healthy short break can be five or ten minutes. If it stretches to twenty or thirty minutes it is not a break, but avoidance behavior or procrastination. It helps to get up and do something active. Get a drink of water, walk around for a bit, get more oxygen to your brain. (Do *not* get on your phone or computer and check out social media!). Set an alarm as a reminder if you need to, but at the end of the break get back to work.

Some people prefer to schedule breaks at set times during the day, or to take a ten minute break every hour for example. I tend to follow the principle of "pay attention to what your body tells you." Whatever the strategy, the goal is to manage mental fatigue so that it does not rob you of productive time and effort.

Plan and Prioritize

One of the underrated benefits of planning and prioritizing well is that it forces you to focus better. Having a plan is more focused than having no plan. Following an agenda is better than jumping around from one thing to another. Prioritizing *is* focusing.

Research suggests that most people can only focus productively on two things at a time maximum, before becoming overwhelmed and unproductive. When it comes to people with ADHD, I strongly recommend focusing on only *one* thing at a time. More than one and the person is simply getting distracted in unproductive ways.

Move While You Think

Moving helps most people think and focus better. This has been a principle well known and practiced throughout recorded history, and perhaps even longer. When people need to focus and think about some important issue in their lives, what do they often do? Go for a walk. This works as well for Fred Jones, wondering about whether to refinance the mortgage, as it did for Bron son of Sarg, wondering about the next wooly mammoth hunt.

Fidgeting is a form of physical restlessness. What some people are surprised to learn is that fidgeting also helps them focus better. Jiggling the foot, tapping the pencil on the desk top – go for it (but be considerate if the behavior is annoying other people around you).

Pacing back and forth in an open space (watch the furniture!) can be helpful when studying or memorizing a large amount of material. It is relaxing, brings more oxygen to the brain to enhance mental alertness, and breaks up the boredom of sitting for a long time. A treadmill or exercise bike provides the same benefits.

Monitor Yourself (How Focused Am I?)

A basic principle for changing or improving any behavior is to monitor the behavior. Paying attention to how well you're paying attention, it turns out, actually helps you pay attention.

Some people find it helpful, a few times per day, to orient themselves to time and task. Pause for a brief moment and ask yourself – am I focused right now? Am I doing what I should be doing?

If the answer is "yes, I am focusing just fine," then continue on. If the answer is "no, I am off task," then take a few moments to re-orient yourself to what you should be doing. Put away any distractions and re-commit to following the agenda on your schedule.

CHAPTER 6

Get Going!

Coping Skills for Reducing Procrastination

"I'LL DO IT LATER" is a very common refrain. Not doing what you *should* be doing, and *continuing* to put off doing it, is something that everyone does occasionally. We all sometimes put off things that we just don't feel like doing right now. We give it a name, procrastination, and treat it like a minor nuisance. No big deal, right?

But what happens if you take that common behavior, the minor nuisance, and put it on steroids (so to speak)? Instead of putting off small and minor things, you also put off large and important things? Instead of procrastinating occasionally, procrastination becomes a way of life that happens on a daily basis, year after year?

What if the procrastination becomes such a chronic problem that you're at risk of failing out of school? Losing your job? Having problems in personal and professional relationships? Now we are describing ADHD level procrastination for many people with ADHD (not everyone). At this high level of intensity procrastination causes serious problems in people's lives. It causes pain. It must be addressed in helpful and constructive ways, and brought down to the level of typical "mild irritant" procrastination.

The Causes of Procrastination

Procrastination is not a unitary phenomenon, but rather is complex behavior. It has both biological and psychological causes. First let us briefly discuss two types of procrastination, *activation difficulty driven procrastination* and *anxiety driven procrastination*. Some people struggle more with one or the other, and some struggle with both. Following this introductory material, the rest of the chapter will focus on specific strategies for reducing and managing procrastination.

Activation Difficulty Driven Procrastination (ADHD)

Activation difficulty is a biological phenomenon that is not exclusive to ADHD, but is more common with ADHD. Simply put, it describes a process where the brain does not get sufficiently excited to initiate behavior and take the first step towards working on a task. In terms of actual behavior the person knows full well they need to get to work and write that report (or do the laundry, call the dentist, unload the dishwasher, etc.). Unfortunately too often the brain reaction is basically "ho hum, I don't feel like it right now, I'll do it later."

The brain literally does not activate sufficiently to initiate goal-directed action. This reaction is driven by biology and neurochemistry – lower levels of dopamine, the neurotransmitter responsible for motivation and reward – and is not a matter of character or personality. The individual might very well be a highly responsible person, he might even have scheduled a time to do laundry, and he knows full well *there are no clean towels or socks left* – but at that point in time you might need to put a gun to his head to get him to start doing laundry. (Some exaggeration of course – it might only take a bow and arrow). The brain simply does not get excited for that task at that point in time.

Activation difficulty is where avoidance behavior and procrastination begin for many people with ADHD. It should also be said that although activation difficulty is one partial *explanation* for excessive procrastination, it should never be used as an *excuse* for excessive procrastination. The individual is still responsible for managing the procrastination so that it does not cause problems for him or her, or for other people in his or her life.

Anxiety Driven Procrastination

Anxiety driven procrastination is avoidance behavior driven by fears, insecurities, and negative thinking. The reaction to a task is not "I just don't feel like doing it," which is so common with activation difficulty. Rather the anxiety reaction is more along the lines of "if I do it I won't get it right, so why even bother trying?" The fear of failure and expectation of disappointment is so strong that the person puts off dealing with the task or project. The end result is the same – procrastination – but due to very different causes.

Anxiety is excessive worry. Negative thinking is often exaggerated and irrational. Even while knowing this, in the moment the person is made very uncomfortable by the anxiety and keeps avoiding and procrastinating. Avoidance behavior of all kinds is more common with anxiety, and in these situations it feeds procrastination.

Approximately 30% of adults with ADHD also have co-existing anxiety. For those who might already be struggling with activation difficulty, anxiety driven procrastination makes the problem with procrastination even more severe.

Anti-Procrastination Strategies

Procrastination is a matter of biology and psychology, and is best managed by addressing it on both levels. What helps on the biology end is increasing levels of the neurotransmitter dopamine. The most reliable methods to increase levels of dopamine in the brain are with aerobic exercise and stimulant medication. Chapter 3 and Chapter 4 in this book discuss ADHD management strategies via exercise programs and medication management.

On the psychological side of managing procrastination the focus needs to be on both cognitive and behavioral strategies. The cognitive approach involves changing patterns of thinking, feeling, and expectations. The behavioral approach involves using hands-on behavior skills and routines.

Reject Excuses and Rationalizations

One of life's simple truths also makes a very effective anti-procrastination mantra: *The best time to do anything is right now.*

"I'll do it later" is an excuse that we tell ourselves to justify why it's okay to *not* do something now. "Later" is just an abstract concept. Later never comes.

When arriving at the decision point about starting or not staring work on a task, make it a conscious decision and take responsibility for it. "I'll do it later" has no place in that decision and should never be accepted as an excuse for not doing it now.

Procrastination is never helpful, but over time many people become very good at making excuses for why it is okay. This excuse-making mindset is hugely counterproductive and must be challenged and resisted.

Another common excuse to make procrastination sound okay is the rationalization that "I work best under pressure." This is simply not true except for very rare situations (e.g., walking a tightrope across a canyon). What the person actually means is that "I work *only* under pressure." The two statements do not mean the same thing. Working under rushed, pressured conditions leads to making more mistakes and doing sub-par work. Don't fool yourself into believing that it is your "best" work.

Expect Success

One of the consequences of years of chronic procrastination is that a person may feels stuck and unable to change. "I'm a procrastinator" becomes a self-fulfilling prophesy. This is a very negative mindset that also must be resisted and changed.

Procrastination is behavior, and behavior can be changed. We are not prisoners of history. The negative expectations of being stuck, being helpless, can also be changed.

These are areas where therapy is best suited to effect positive change. Changing old ways of thinking and old behavior patterns takes some work, but so what? Get to work. And that feeling of being stuck? It's just a feeling.

Be Productive, Not Perfect

The anxiety driven form of procrastination is based on the fear of "it won't be good enough." I know it won't be good enough, the person thinks, so I won't bother trying. I know I will fail, so I don't want to think about it or deal with it right now. I'll get to it later.

A related fear is that the work won't live up to someone else's expectations (real or imagined), and that person will react with disapproval or criticism. The negative thinking creates more anxiety, which leads to more avoidance behavior and procrastination.

One way to combat the fear of "not good enough" is to give oneself permission to not be perfect. Be imperfect, it's okay – and welcome to where most of us live. Acknowledge the anxiety, then take the first step anyway. It's a battle that must be fought, and when it is fought it will be won. If the anxiety is intense it should be addressed as an anxiety issue, and again some therapy may be helpful.

Embrace Structure (And Resist Structure Aversion)

Having a plan, a strategy, or a routine does not guarantee that you will not procrastinate on a task or a project – but it could give you a fighting chance. Many people with ADHD have a love/hate relationship with structure. They know that it's necessary, and have seen the benefits from it at times, but dread the feeling of being *too* structured or organized.

Some people look at a page in their planner, that for example outlines their agenda for Tuesday, and they shudder. All those lines that separate blocks of time look like the bars of a jail cell to them. They feel trapped. Ughh! I call that feeling structure aversion.

Some people look at a page in their planner and don't see jail bars, but a road map. The structured times and items on their agenda are vehicles on Follow Through Avenue. As long as they stay and keep driving on Follow Through Avenue they will reach the final destination, which might be called A Good Day's Work Plaza. Structure promotes better focusing, staying on track, and consistency.

For every person, ADHD or no ADHD, the mindset that we choose (and it is a *choice*) about structure makes all the difference. Do you treat it as a jail cell and do your best to avoid it? Or do you treat it like a road map and embrace it? If you keep getting lost in the wilderness, I strongly recommend the road map approach.

Plan and Schedule It

A task or project that is planned out in detail, and scheduled on a timeline, is more likely to get done than one that is not. This is making use of basic planning and time management. The old saying that football coaches are fond of repeating – "if you fail to plan, you plan to fail" – applies to more than just football.

Be clear on what you need to do, how you're going to do it, and when you're going to do it. Visualize the finished product in your mind. What will it look like? How will you feel when it's completed? How will you feel if it does *not* get done?

If the task is a simple thing that you can do now, do it now. If it's a bigger project, do the planning and schedule time for working on it. When you make time for a project you make it a priority. Things that are not prioritized tend to get put off for "later."

When you schedule something give yourself a set time, including a specific start time. "This weekend" is not a set time. Saturday afternoon from 2:00 PM to 4:00 PM is a set time. Put it in your planner to have a reminder, and do not let other things distract you during that allocated time (actual emergencies tend to be few and far between).

In the example above, commit to 2:00 PM as your start time – and *hit it*. Not 2:15 or 2:30 or 3:00 PM, but 2:00 PM sharp. Remember your start time and keep it holy. Make it a matter of pride and principle.

Chunk It

Chunking is the strategy of taking a large task or project and breaking it down into smaller, more manageable pieces. It can be very effective for dealing with both types of procrastination, whether activation difficulty based or anxiety based.

How do you eat an elephant? One spoonful at a time.

If you've been avoiding cleaning up your messy basement, and procrastinating for months now, and you really know you should but it's such a huge mess – chunk it. Don't make the goal to clean your basement, which might take days and makes you dread the very thought of it. Make the goal to clean one-fourth of your basement. If that is still dread-inducing, make the goal to clean one-eighth of your basement.

Still dread-inducing? Make a goal to spend 30 minutes on cleaning your basement at 2:00 PM on Saturday afternoon. Chunk the task down to small enough pieces so that no possible excuse of "I'll do it later" would be acceptable.

Increase the Entertainment Factor

Getting started on the boring, routine stuff (e.g., cleaning your basement) is when activation difficulty associated with ADHD becomes a real challenge. It is not possible to fool your brain and react as if cleaning the basement is actually a "fun" activity. What is possible however is to find some ways to make the boring project less boring.

Treat yourself to your favorite beverage. Put on your favorite music. The more you can add an entertainment factor, the more you can reduce the boredom factor and thus decrease the activation difficulty. The goal is to make what feels painfully boring into "normal" boring. Then get to work.

Increase the Social Factor

One tried and true method to make something that is very boring less boring is to have some company while doing it. This is true for two reasons. First, having company adds to the entertainment factor and makes the activity more pleasant. It is easier to stick with a workout schedule, for example, if you have a workout buddy. In the example of cleaning the basement, having someone helping with the chore helps reduce the boredom factor.

A second reason why having company helps is due to the "body double" phenomenon. This is part of basic human biology and works the same for all people. Simply having someone else close by provides a comfort level, and also helps with motivation and focusing. This works for an adult cleaning the basement, and works equally well for a child sitting at the dining room table doing her homework.

CHAPTER 7

Don't Forget!

Memory Management Tools
and Strategies

MANY PEOPLE WITH ADHD (not everyone) are simply more forgetful than most people. This is not related to intelligence, personality, general health, or any other factor. It is a basic part of ADHD biology.

If we were to gather a large enough sample of people who fit the "absent minded professor" stereotype, there is a very good chance that many would also fit the ADHD behavioral profile when it comes to forgetfulness. How can a person who just wrote a brilliant business proposal walk into the next room to get something – and forget what she went to get?

How does George have a very efficient and productive day at work – but forgets to pick up his son after baseball practice even though his wife reminded him this morning: "George don't forget to pick up Tommy after baseball practice!"

Everyone forgets occasionally. As with every ADHD "symptom," people with ADHD simply do it a lot more. When it happens excessively it starts to cause problems, and then it needs to be managed better. Managed poorly, it can create difficulties in jobs, relationships, and sometimes simply managing the basic tasks of daily living.

There is no "cure" for forgetfulness. ADHD medications are not memory pills. For that matter, we do not have memory pills. Supplements such as ginkgo biloba, ginseng, omega-3 fatty acids, and various types of herbs and vitamins sometimes provide marginal benefits for general cognitive functioning. The omega-3 oils are good for promoting general brain health, and certainly are worth taking for that reason, but should not be considered to be any kind of special treatment for improving memory. Medications designed to treat Alzheimer's disease are not appropriate or effective for use with the general population.

The most effective way to manage ADHD forgetfulness is behaviorally. This means developing and using a system of organization and reminders. It is not very exciting but it is helpful, and essential to preventing problems that can be caused by forgetfulness (e.g., picking up Tommy after baseball practice).

Three Types of Memory

ADHD affects short-term memory, long-term memory, and working memory. Managing forgetfulness in each area requires a somewhat different approach.

- *Short-term memory* is generally considered to cover a very short period of time lasting approximately 15 to 30 seconds.

  o This is the type of memory that, for example, allows you to look at a phone number and remember the number as you are dialing it.

  o ADHD biology can make this type of task more challenging. It may be necessary to look at only three or four numbers at a time, and dial only three or four numbers before looking back.

  o In the example of going to the next room to get something and forgetting what you were supposed to get, ADHD distractibility also becomes an issue. In the time it takes to get from here to there the person's mind might easily have wandered to one or two other things.

- *Long-term memory* covers information that is stored in the brain, but may either be simply forgotten or not consistently available for recall.

  o George forgetting to pick up Tommy after the baseball game, for example.

  o George, in the moment, not remembering the name of a colleague as she walks up to greet him. He *knows* her name, but it just doesn't "click" at that moment. Of course one minute later it clicks – Linda!

o George has a spotty memory of his child-hood. This is not to pick on George – it is a common occurrence for many adults with ADHD. *This is completely unrelated to intelligence or other factors.*

o The only way to improve long-term memory retention and recall is to review. And review. And review. This is particularly important for students of all ages (from elementary school to medical school) who need to learn and remember a great deal of information.

• *Working memory* refers to organizing and arranging multiple bits of information in your mind, recalling the information as needed, and following a sequence.

o Good working memory is essential for multi-tasking.

o **Fact #1 about multi-tasking**: *nobody* is good at it. Some people take pride in claiming "I am good at multi-tasking," however chances are very high that they are fooling themselves. What the research on multi-tasking shows is that it actually decreases efficiency and productivity.

o **Fact #2 about multi-tasking:** if you are a person with ADHD, *don't even think about it.* What may look like multi-tasking is most likely just being distracted and scattered.

o Some jobs require a good deal of multi-tasking – an office receptionist processing written information while also answering the phones, for example – and those jobs might create more challenges for some individuals with ADHD.

o If you have a choice in the matter, it is strongly recommended to work on being a very efficient single-tasker. Focus on only one thing at a time, and finish what you start.

Behavioral Strategies for Managing Forgetfulness

It is worth repeating (again!) that managing the biology of ADHD well requires taking care of yourself well. The benefits of exercise, sleep, and nutrition apply to memory functioning as much as to any other aspect of health and brain functions.

Sleep deprivation is very bad for memory functioning. So is failing to maintain a healthy blood sugar level. A program of aerobic exercise provides benefits for brain functioning across the board, including memory functioning. Please refer to Chapter 3 for a more detailed discussion of these factors.

The behavioral management of forgetfulness requires systems and routines. The process takes some work and stick-to-it consistency, but the benefits are undeniable.

Use One Integrated System for Planning and Reminders

I have yet to meet an adult with ADHD who can keep track of time-sensitive tasks (appointments, lunches, meetings, etc.) without using some type of planner on a daily or near daily basis.

The particular type of planner does not matter. Digital or hard copy is fine; some people are more comfortable with one or the other. The planner must have two essential features. First, it should have a calendar function with days, dates, and hours formatted in. Second, it should be portable so that it goes where you go. It must be available for instant input of information, and for checking and instant retrieval of information.

I am sometimes asked the question "what is the best planner?" My answer is always the same: the one that you will use and stick with. Get one that feels comfortable to you. The biggest problem with planners is when they don't feel comfortable or don't provide the level of functionality the person needs. That is a planner that is soon put aside and forgotten.

"If it's Worth Remembering, It's Worth Writing Down"

This is one ADHD mantra that is worth remembering and living by. It does not matter how bright, creative, or responsible you are, if you have ADHD most likely you cannot trust your memory to keep track of all the things you need to remember. That includes the conference call at 11:00 AM, lunch with Ted at 12:30 PM, and yes also picking up Tommy after baseball practice at 4:30 PM.

If it's worth remembering, it's worth writing down. In this case "writing down" means putting it into your organizational system. Time-sensitive tasks go into your planner, listed at the appropriate day and time. Small tasks that you need to remember and get to eventually (e.g., buy a flea collar for the dog) can go on a task list.

The combination of calendar and task list work well together. Use both to input information and give yourself reminders. Check them on a regular basis.

"A Place for Everything, And Everything in Its Place"

This is another ADHD mantra that is worth remembering and living by. Many people waste a great deal of time looking for items that they use frequently, because they simply don't remember where they put them. These include keys, wallets, phones, phone chargers, insurance cards, materials for work, and so on.

The only solution for the "where is my (fill in the blank)" problem is to assign a home location for frequently used items – and put them there when you are not using them. That means, for example, when you get home and walk in the door your keys go on a key hook (or another assigned location). They don't go in your jeans pocket, or jacket pocket, or the kitchen counter, or on the bedroom dresser.

This is a very basic but effective strategy. Make it a routine and waste less time looking for your stuff.

Keep Things in the Open (Avoid "Out Of Sight, Out Of Mind")

The "out of sight, out of mind" phenomenon is occasionally a problem for everyone. For people with ADHD it's like kryptonite. Combine living in the moment with forgetfulness, and some important things that we need to deal with (e.g., that bill in the desk drawer) simply disappear from awareness. What bill in the desk drawer? Oh yes, this one, the one you came across two weeks after it was due.

As a rule of thumb, keeping things you need to get to out in the open works better than putting them away. Bookshelves work better than file drawers. Letter trays work better than putting mail somewhere out of sight. Visual reminders are just as important as auditory reminders (e.g., an alarm on your phone, your spouse complaining again, etc.).

Storing things in see-through containers works on the same principle. Pack your favorite winter sweater in a cardboard box and you might not see it again for four or five years. Put it in a see-through plastic container and you are much more likely to see it when the weather turns cold again.

Keep an Errand Container by the Door or In Your Car

Many people with busy schedules (i.e., most of us) need to make time for running errands – the small stuff that we get to when we get to it. Return a purchased item to a store, for example, or drop off a jacket to the dry cleaners.

Keeping some sort of errand container (a box works best) around helps to organize the materials you might need for your errand runs. It also helps you remember to get to those things when you go on your errand run.

CHAPTER 8

De-clutter Your Home and Work Environment

LIVING WITH CLUTTER IS a common experience for many people. Some are comfortable with it as long as it's not causing any major problems. For some it is a chronic source of irritation.

Let it be said once again that it is a misconception to believe that people with ADHD are not capable of organization. They are very capable of organizing a room, a house, or an office, for example. In many cases the issue is simply that they don't want to be bothered. Organization is one of those "boring" things that get neglected. There are so many other more interesting things to do!

Having a cluttered or disorganized environment isn't a problem – until it is. At some point the pain cost of being disorganized becomes too high and the person gets motivated to clean things up. Often this leads to a flurry of cleaning, organizing, and putting things away. Success!

Usually, a week later, the old messes and clutter are back again.

Think "Clutter Prevention" (Not Clutter Clean-Up)

Consistency requires structure. The way to get off the roller coaster of cleaning up messes, making more messes, and cleaning up the new messes – is to stop making new messes. That is not as hard as it might sound. It does require developing a system of organization and sticking with it.

If the goal is to maintain a reasonably well organized environment at home or at work, some systems and routines will be required. This is an unavoidable fact of life for everyone.

Every Item Needs a "Home"

This strategy was mentioned previously in the chapter on memory management. It applies equally well in creating a system for clutter prevention.

Step one in developing a system for organizing your space is to decide what items you actually want and need to have around. Step two is to decide where those items belong – the "home location." Step three is to put the items there when they are not in use.

If you don't have enough space to assign where an item should belong, it's possible that you simply have too much stuff.

When You Have More Stuff than Space

Stuff accumulates. If you live somewhere long enough chances are that you have a collection of things that you never use, don't have room for, or both. In that situation the solution is to purge selectively. Take one room at a time, go through the items in the room and decide what you want to keep. The items you don't need to keep should be placed in one of three categories:

- *Throw away.* Keep a garbage can or garbage bag handy and toss whatever has no value away. That magazine that's two months old? Garbage. That cheap ink pen or pencil stub that you never use? Garbage.

- *Donate.* Keep a box handy for items that you don't need but might have value to other people. That set of cookware in the kitchen cabinet that you never use, for example.

- *Long-term storage.* Some items have no immediate functional use, but you want to hang on to them. Often these have sentimental value. Assuming that you have a space for long-term storage, transfer those items there. Many people overdo this, to the point of renting a long-term storage locker that gets filled with stuff – which they never see or use again.

What to Keep? What to Throw Away?

Items that you keep in your home or work environment should have either a clear functional purpose or a decorative purpose. Functional means you actually use it and it provides some benefits.

When purging, throw away items that fall into these categories:

- *No functional purpose.* People keep things around that they *might* need at some point in the future, for example that microwave poached egg maker that your sister gave you for your birthday.

- *Not used recently.* The rule of thumb is, if you have not used an item in the past 12 months chances are very low that you will use it again. This applies to your clothes closet, kitchen, office, and other places where you live or work. There's a name for all that stuff that's just sitting around – clutter.

- *Multiples.* This applies to accumulating more items of the same type than you actually use or need. How many spatulas do you have in your kitchen drawer? Most people do fine with one or two, but some accumulate half a dozen. How many coffee mugs do you need? Having a few around is functional; having a kitchen cabinet full might be excessive. Excessive multiples are clutter.

Time to Call in the Cavalry? Hire a Professional Organizer

If setting up a system of organization seems too daunting, or if you simply want some expert help in doing it, consider hiring a professional organizer. These folks help people get organized for a living, and they are good at it.

A professional organizer will come to your home or place of business, scope out the messy situation (don't worry, she or he has seen worse!), discuss your goals, and then give you a plan of action. Most professional organizers will do the hands-on work with you, first designing the system of what goes where and why, then doing the actual work with you of getting things into place.

CHAPTER 9

Improve Time Management, Planning, and Prioritizing

MOST PEOPLE WITH ADHD have a binary sense of time. The most urgent sense of time, and honestly the only one that feels relevant, is best described as "now." Anything that does not fall under the current experience of "now" falls into a distant and vague notion of "later." This goes a long ways towards explaining why people live in the moment and react to the immediate. Time does not have much "depth" to it. "Now" is the only priority, the rest is a foggy unknown that doesn't get much if any attention.

This biological explanation does not mean that people with ADHD cannot manage time well. ADHD should never be used as an excuse for failing to look ahead and plan well, or for habitually running late because of underestimating how long it takes to get somewhere. Individuals with ADHD can do well with managing time -- it just takes a little extra work.

Improving one's sense of time and managing time well can be done with the help of a variety of systems and routines. Following are some examples.

Make Time Visual

Many people with ADHD report that their sense of time improves when they can "see" time. Actually this phenomenon helps everyone, but individuals with ADHD get an even greater benefit from it.

Using some kind of planner, hard copy or digital, is essential to making time visual. You want to be able to see your day, with all the hourly time blocks and all the items on your schedule. See your week. See your month. Making time visual simply provides more perspective and makes time feel more "real." It makes planning easier, including estimating and allocating time for tasks and projects.

Learn to Estimate Time Better (The 1.5 Rule)

Two factors work against people with ADHD when it comes to estimating time accurately. Luckily both factors can be overcome with awareness and some coping skills. First, as mentioned above, time awareness does not come naturally. This is pure biology. Second, in my experience many people with ADHD are eternal optimists. This is part of their emotionality.

The end result is chronic underestimating of how long things take due to over-optimistic expectations. Sure, Merle says to herself, I can finish that paper in three hours – although realistically it will take six or more. Sure, Randall says to himself, I can get to my dentist appointment in 15 minutes – although realistically it will take 30 minutes. This explains why Merle turns in papers late, and why Randall is habitually 10 or 15 minutes late. Even though it frustrates them it keeps happening.

The solution to solving the problem of underestimating time is to *not* trust your sense of time. It does not matter how smart or responsible you are. If you have ADHD chances are that your brain will fool you and you will underestimate how much time you need to (fill in the blank). And the next thing you know you are late for your dentist appointment – again!

An elegantly simple strategy for estimating time more accurately is to use the 1.5 rule. However much time you think you need to get something done or to get somewhere, multiply that time by 1.5. If you think you need two hours to write that report, schedule three hours. If you think you need 30 minutes to get somewhere, give yourself 45 minutes.

The 1.5 rule works so well for people who use it and stick with it, it's almost spooky. The only way it doesn't work is if people stop using it. In order to work consistently it must become a routine and be used consistently.

Experience being the best teacher, some people find that 1.5 time still leaves them a bit short. In that situation it is perfectly fine to convert it to a 2.0 rule. What works for you is what works for you. This principle also applies to academic accommodations, for example when requesting extended time testing. Most people do fine with 1.5 time, but some need 2.0 time.

Use Planners and Calendars like A General

Time management cannot be done efficiently without using a planner. This applies to all people with a busy lifestyle, and it is *critical* for most people with ADHD. Without a planner, a realistic schedule, and some consistent routines, people tend to be scattered and jump from one thing to another. That is the recipe for being unproductive. That old saying about inefficiency -- "*The best way to get nothing done is to try to do everything at once*" – becomes a way of life.

Everyone over the age of 15 can use a personal planner for managing her or his schedule (the sooner you start the better). When it comes to time management and family life, a separate family calendar that is posted for everyone to see can also be very helpful. ("George, don't forget to pick up Tommy after baseball practice" will work much better if it is also posted on the family calendar and George's personal planner). Many businesses use team calendars or project calendars.

Most people follow a set work schedule, which makes it easier because that is external structure. Follow the schedule and show up for work on time. If you are self-employed, it is imperative that you create your own work schedule and stick to it.

The activities that require structure and scheduling in your planner are the daily and weekly routines of personal and family life. Even more specifically, the activities that get scheduled in your planner should *only* be the priorities that you determine are important enough to have a time allocated to them. Do *not* schedule every hour of the day in your planner (more on that later).

Some essential routines that need a schedule in order to be consistent:

- *Workout schedule.* If you're going to commit to an exercise routine it needs a schedule. Certain days at certain times, and follow the routine as best you can. It does not need to be followed perfectly (not possible in the real world) – it only needs to promote consistency.

- *Sleep schedule.* Schedule a regular bedtime with a bedtime routine. The problems caused by sleep deprivation have been discussed already in other chapters in this book. A sleep schedule helps promote consistent and healthy sleep.

- *Meal schedule.* If you are not eating meals on a regular basis and are not maintaining a healthy blood sugar level, it is worthwhile to schedule meal times in your planner. Some people "forget" to eat breakfast, or are "too busy" to eat lunch. Making time for meals in your planner helps prevent those problems.

Some optional routines that need a schedule in order to be consistent are listed below. Again, prioritize and be selective. The routines that go in your planner are the routines that *you* need to be consistent with.

- *Grocery shopping.* Not buying groceries on a regular basis means not having healthy food in the house means eating a lot more junk food and fast food. Scheduling a time to grocery shop once a week prevents that problem. Ordering groceries online to be delivered works great also – it just needs a scheduled time to become a routine.

- *Laundry.* Few people enjoy doing laundry. If you schedule a time for it, you increase the chances that it will become a routine. Wednesday night is laundry night – what fun! (Increase the entertainment factor -- treat yourself to watching a movie, play a video game, enjoy your favorite beverage, etc.).

- *Cleaning.* Another boring activity that needs a routine to have any consistency. Even 30 minutes of cleaning twice a week will go a long ways towards cleaning up small messes and do wonders for your clutter-prevention strategy.

- *Paying bills.* Whatever bills are not being paid via automatic payments need a regular time during the week (or month) to get paid. No one likes late fee charges.

Leave Blank Space in Your Schedule

The biggest problem when it comes to ADHD and time management is failing to schedule. The second biggest problem is overscheduling. Somewhere between the two extremes there exists a healthy balance. Where that balance point is for you is unique to you. Find it.

It is not necessary, and indeed not realistic or healthy, to fill your planner with scheduled activities all day long, seven days a week. I strongly discourage it. An over-booked schedule feels overwhelming and oppressive. It's impossible to stick to, leads to feelings of frustration and failure, and often leads to abandoning the planner because "this doesn't work!"

A much better strategy is to only schedule things that are priorities for you, and leave blank space in between. Some things to keep in mind:

- *Blank space is your friend.* Leaving blank space in your planner is not an indication of "slacking" or underachieving. It a productive strategy. Be okay with it. Resist any urges for guilt-tripping.

- *Leave flex time in your schedule.* Things almost never take exactly as long as we plan for them. Leave at least 30 minutes of blank space – flex time – between scheduled items. If you finish earlier, great. Do something else or just take a break. Flex time will help prevent one scheduled activity from running into another.

- *Schedule breaks.* The ADHD mind, which trends towards getting distracted, gets mentally fatigued faster when engaged in tasks that require sustained mental effort (apologies for sounding like a textbook, but the statement is accurate). For some people scheduling a 15 minute break mid-morning and mid-afternoon can be helpful in preventing mental fatigue. As mentioned in previous chapters, taking short breaks of five or ten minutes, as needed, is also a good idea. Taking breaks *when needed* works better than trudging on when you are unfocused and unproductive.

- *Leave one day free on your schedule.* Ideally it is much healthier to have one day during the week that is free time. This is the "blank space" day on your calendar. Use it for relaxation, social time, family time, hobbies, or just bumming around the house or apartment. It does wonders for stress management and maintaining a healthy and balanced schedule. And if you start guilt-tripping about taking a day off, it is worth remembering the wise advice given by my grandmother: "If it was good enough for God, it's good enough for you."

Give Yourself an "Out the Door" Time

One reason many people with ADHD tend to be late getting to places is because they habitually underestimate how long it actually takes to get there. The 1.5 rule discussed earlier helps prevent this problem.

Another reason people tend to be late is because they get distracted and delay leaving on time. This is sometimes referred to as the "one more thing" phenomenon. I need to leave, but first let me load the dishwasher. First let me check my email. Time flies and now you're running 15 or 20 minutes late.

The solution to the "one more thing" phenomenon is to set a strict out-the-door time and hit it. If you have a 2:00 PM appointment, and it takes 20 minutes to get there, then 1:40 PM is your out-the-door time. At 1:35 get ready to leave, and at 1:40 sharp out the door. There are no short-cuts and no way around this. Setting an alarm can be helpful as a reminder and an auditory cue.

Are You Inefficient? Or Overcommitted?

For most people there are two major reasons for feeling overwhelmed. One is caused by being inefficient, which might be related to poor time management and low productivity. The solution for this particular problem is to improve productivity.

A second major reason many people feel overwhelmed is because they simply take on too much. They are over-committed. The only solution for taking on too much is to cut back. There are limits to improving efficiency.

For a variety of reasons many people with ADHD are prone to becoming overcommitted – which is followed by feeling overwhelmed. It is important to be clear on the nature of the problem in order to find the right solution.

In the case of being chronically overcommitted there needs to be a recalibration of expectations and responsibilities. There needs to be an effort to resist jumping to "yes" every time a new interesting and exciting idea comes along. There needs to be diligent use of one's planner, and balancing one's schedule in a realistic and healthy way.

Peter Jaksa

CHAPTER 10

ADHD and Relationships

GETTING ALONG WITH PEOPLE is something that many individuals with ADHD do quite well. The energy, spontaneity, empathy, humor, and creativity that is common to many people with ADHD create a certain level of charm that comes across in a positive way to other people. Many adults with ADHD are attracted to each other on the basis of these positive personal qualities.

The personal qualities that make a person with ADHD a fun date can also make her or him a very loving spouse, partner, or parent. As is often the case, in a marriage or other long-term relationship some less positive aspects of ADHD biology can and do cause difficulties and challenges at times. These are not typically insurmountable challenges, but they may need some work. Just like any other relationships.

ADHD-specific challenges can be dealt with. However, first they need to be acknowledged and understood. Procrastinating on cleaning the garage for six months can drive both partners batty. Forgetting to pick up Tommy after baseball practice may turn into a minor crisis, and also may start an argument when George gets home. And for good reason.

Let's be very clear about one thing: *it is always the responsibility of the person with ADHD to be responsible for their own behavior and to do what they need to do.* Responsible people do not make excuses, and ADHD should *never* be used as an excuse for not fulfilling one's responsibilities. Just like everyone else.

Common Issues in Personal Relationships

Difficulty Listening and Paying Attention

An individual with a high level of distractibility is more likely to "zone out" during a conversation. This is pure biology, not volitional behavior. Problems arise if the other partner interprets the behavior as a sign of indifference or disrespect. Hey, I'm talking to you – don't you care about what I have to say?

The fact of the matter is that the person does care, but there will be times when his or her mind will wander. When that happens simply point it out, and she or he will "snap out of it" and be attentive again. Understanding the biology of distractibility helps in not taking the behavior personally and feeling slighted or rejected.

Another communication issue that can cause bad feelings and friction is when the person frequently interrupts in conversation. This leads to "talking over" the other person.

This impulsive behavior is sometimes caused by the ADHD partner getting excited about an idea or thought they want to express – and boom, can't wait, out it comes! At times the ADHD partner may be worried that they will forget what they want to say – and bam, they just go ahead and say it.

If these behaviors get irritating over time, as can happen with any couple and irritating behavior, they should be treated as communication issues and addressed accordingly. As always, the partner with ADHD should be responsible and considerate and make efforts to be attentive (see Chapter 5) and to tone down the impulsivity (see Chapter 14).

Trouble Completing Tasks

Not following through and doing what one is expected to do always create feelings of frustration. Sometimes it leads to resentment and anger. Knowing that a person keeps their promises is one of the foundations of trust.

In every relationship each person is responsible for following through and doing her or his share of the work. This may be as simple as taking out the garbage on a regular basis, or as complicated as planning next year's vacation trip to Europe. Do what you agree to do.

Problems arise when one person is not consistent in doing their share. A common pattern is that the other partner becomes the one who has to remind often, then eventually nag, then perhaps occasionally threaten. In a very toxic dynamic the partners take on a parent-child role. This must be avoided at all costs because eventually it kills a relationship.

Do what you need to do to get your stuff done. No excuses and no way around it.

Forgetfulness

Everyone forgets. People with ADHD tend to be more forgetful than most people. This is also pure biology, however that does not make it any less frustrating when it keeps happening excessively. Two things can help, one to a small degree and one to a very large degree.

What can help to a small degree is for the non-ADHD partner to be careful not to interpret forgetfulness on the part of the person with ADHD as a lack of caring or lack of commitment to the relationship. It is not uncommon for someone to think "if you cared about me, you would have remembered" – however this applies poorly when dealing with a partner with ADHD. Forgetfulness is biology, and it is not related to intelligence or caring.

What can help to a very large degree (and really is the only solution to this problem) is for the partner with ADHD to work diligently on designing and then *using* a system of organization and reminders (see Chapter 7, "Don't Forget!"). Do that, and important things are not forgotten or neglected. It is the only responsible way to manage forgetfulness.

Emotional Overreaction

The level of emotionality for many people with ADHD is simply higher than for people in the general population. That can be a double-edged sword. On the positive side it can make people more caring, more loving, more passionate about things that interest them, and more committed to things they believe in.

On the negative side, it can make some people more likely to overreact emotionally. That might mean that people get upset too easily, are irritated or bothered by minor things, or lose their temper too quickly. Some people have a greater sensitivity to criticism, disapproval, or rejection. Very emotional people react very emotionally.

One solution to emotional over-reactivity is to de-fuse when possible, and also to refuse to escalate. This might mean acknowledging the upset feelings but then, if the anger persists, distancing from it. Ask that you take some time to cool down and then discuss the matter. One positive thing about ADHD emotionality is that while people are likely to get upset quickly, they are also likely to get over it quickly.

Not Staying in Touch With Old Friends (And New)

"Out of sight, out of mind" is a problem that applies to friends as well as objects and tasks. Many people with ADHD get so caught up in the present they don't think about taking the time to call or write old friends, plan a get together, send a birthday card, and so on. Making friends? Easy. Maintaining friendships? More difficult.

Common Issues in Professional Relationships

Procrastination

Procrastination is always perceived by supervisors and co-workers as irresponsible, unmotivated, and simply "lazy." It has no redeeming positive qualities. It hurts productivity for the individual, and for the team the person is working on. If excessive, it gets people fired.

Strategies for reducing and managing procrastination are discussed in depth in Chapter 6 ("Get Going!") so will not be repeated here. If it is a recurring problem it needs to be managed better. No excuses.

Difficulties with Planning and Organization

A disorganized workplace is not only bad for efficiency and productivity, but is viewed by many as an indication of a sloppy and uncaring attitude. Inconsistent and disorganized effort, jumping around from one thing to another, shows lack of planning and discipline and is always viewed as unprofessional.

There is no reason to settle for being disorganized and unproductive at work. Chapter 8 and Chapter 9 cover strategies for improving organization and time management.

Lack of Punctuality

Late for meetings. Late in completing tasks. Late for lunch. I'm late, I'm late, I'm late...

Tardiness always comes across in a negative way. Yes, even if people joke about it. It often inconveniences other people, and always looks irresponsible. If lack of punctuality is a chronic problem it may be time to do more work on time management skills (see Chapter 9).

Being Intrusive or Disruptive

Most people with ADHD do not tolerate boredom well. As children they might become the "class clown," or disrupt the class by excessive talking to other people around them. As adults, sometimes these social and disruptive behaviors pop up in a work setting. It is imperative to be attentive to social cues that indicate the person in question does not welcome the attention at that point in time.

CHAPTER 11

Parenting a Child
With ADHD

CHILDREN WITH ADHD OFTEN need extra care and attention from parents, teachers, daycare workers, and other caretakers in their lives. Young children who are hyperactive need more careful monitoring to make sure they don't get themselves into situations where they might get hurt. An older child might need some extra attention and effort to keep busy and actively engaged in things that interest her or him. A child in elementary school or middle school might need some extra help in getting organized and keeping track of things, making sure assignments get turned in, and coordinating efforts between teachers and parents.

To which my question is – so what? It is almost comical how many books written for parents of children with ADHD start out with the message that "parenting a child with ADHD is so very *hard*, you poor parents deserve a medal!" To which I say: hogwash. Also, pure unadulterated nonsense. Who ever said parenting was supposed to be simple and easy? Beyond that, let's not put these children into a different category of children. They're just children.

Maintaining a healthy perspective is important. The child with ADHD did not "catch" ADHD out of pure thin air. Statistically there is a very strong probability that one or both parents, or one or more grandparents, also have ADHD (sometimes it skips generations, depending on the genetic load). If ADHD biology is part of your family genetic history, the most constructive way to deal with it is to accept it, understand it, and take responsibility for helping the child to manage it well.

Secondly, know that most children with ADHD eventually grow up into reasonably productive and reasonably happy adults. Just like everyone else. Do not allow the disorder-mongers and mental illness purveyors to convince you that your child is somehow a different species of child, doomed to failure and unhappiness. That is also pure unadulterated nonsense.

Each child with ADHD is a unique individual, with unique strengths and weaknesses, and a unique personality. Each will make his or her own way in life, to different levels of success and happiness.

The goal for parents and educators is to help those children with ADHD manage age-appropriate responsibilities, learn in school, get along with and make friends with their peers, and mature along with their peers as they get older. Just like all children.

Children with ADHD need the same basic things that all children need – and sometimes they need a little more. All children need structure and routines, but children with ADHD may need it more. All children need to be taught organization skills, but kids with ADHD may need to work harder and longer at developing them. All children need consistency with respect to study schedules, morning routines, and bedtime routines, but many children with ADHD need it more.

Developing efficient systems of organization and other productivity skills does not end when childhood ends. That is an ongoing process that lasts into adulthood for all people who care about being productive. The goal with all children, whether or not they have ADHD, is to help them build a solid foundation before they reach adulthood. Below are some strategies that could be helpful.

Maintain Realistic Expectations and Provide Appropriate Assistance

One of the leading gurus of the disorder model of ADHD decided a long time ago that children with ADHD are developmentally and emotionally delayed by an average of three years compared to their peers. This now appears to be accepted as gospel truth by many professionals working in the ADHD field.

In my experience this is painting with a brush that is much too broad. Some children are slower to mature, many are not, and some are precocious and more mature than their age peers.

It is true that some (not all) children with ADHD are slower to develop emotional self-control, but that comes with the territory of having a high level of emotionality as part of one's basic biology. Some children take longer to develop organization and time management skills, which comes with the biological territory of having a poor sense of time and poor sense of the passage of time.

These are common features of ADHD biology, and not necessarily "developmental delays" that cause any significant problems. As every parent knows, different children develop at their own pace in different areas of growth and development. It is not a race. Stereotyping children with ADHD as being three years behind their peers in emotional and cognitive development is inaccurate and terribly unhelpful.

What is important in parenting or educating any child is to take the maturity level and skills level of that particular child into consideration. It is frustrating for all involved to expect a child to do what that child is not yet capable of doing. For example, one of the most unhelpful messages to parents from educators is that "he (or she) is old enough to do that by himself (or herself) by now."

No, it is not a matter of age or maturity level. If a particular child needs more help to get more consistent with routines and other organization skills, for example, then provide what that child needs for as long as necessary to develop and maintain those behavioral skills.

Co-ordinate Strategies and Services with Teachers, Principals, and School Counselors

The large majority of children with ADHD do not need special education services. As mentioned above, some will benefit from more individualized attention and behavior skills training. Often this can be done on an informal basis, particularly with children in the early grades, based on discussions between parents and teachers.

If a broader range of services or more structured plan might be needed, request to have the school conduct a formal 504 evaluation. This involves an assessment to determine the child's educational needs with input from a team of school staff. Parents contribute to this process along with teachers, school counselors, the principal or other administrators, and possibly the school psychologist if psychological or psychoeducational testing is called for.

Win the Battle of the Messy Bedroom.

In the modern history of parent-child relationships, few verbal exchanges have sparked as much complaining and arguing as "clean your room." While parents should of course be realistic about age-appropriate responsibilities, they need not put up with utter chaos either. Even very young children can handle simple tasks such as putting away their toys, with assistance.

The golden rule for maintaining order in a child's room is that everything has a place where it belongs. Things that don't have a place (or don't get put there after being used) end up in the ubiquitous pile of clutter. If there's no room for an item to have its own place, it belongs in the basement, attic, storage shed, or recycling bin—anywhere but the child's room.

Helping a Child Manage Clutter

- Assign every object in a child's room a designated "home" location. This is where things are put when they are not being used.

- Establish a daily, five or ten minute routine for a child to tidy his or her room. This is when all toys, clothes, books, and other items are returned to their "home" locations.
- At least every few months, help your child sort and purge unneeded possessions. (Rarely used items that are keepers should be placed on shelves or in storage.)
- Provide reminders, gentle pushes and supervision, but don't do the child's work if the child is capable of doing it.
- Be positive and supportive, not critical. Staying organized takes extra effort for many kids with ADHD, and sometimes it gets frustrating, but that is no reason to give up the effort.

The Magic of Routines

All children benefit from routines to promote consistent behavior. Not every activity needs to be (or should be) turned into a routine. They are most helpful for accomplishing common tasks (e.g., brush your teeth before going to bed) and keeping daily life manageable. Below are some of the most basic and helpful routines.

The "Get Out the Door" Morning Routine

- "Rise and shine" at a regular time and head straight for the bathroom.
- Wash face, comb hair, brush teeth, etc.
- Get dressed with the clothing that was picked out the night before.
- Eat a healthy breakfast (with the TV, computer, and other distractions turned off).

- Put on a jacket or coat if needed, and grab the school bag which should be all packed and waiting by the door.
- Walk out the door at an established "out the door" time.

The Homework Routine

- Since many children with ADHD need a mental break after school, allow at least 30 minutes to an hour of downtime for playing or watching TV.
- Establish a regular place and time for doing homework
- To help with the transition to doing homework, give the child a calm reminder 10 minutes prior to the study time.
- Help the child review the assignments to be worked on and make sure needed materials are handy.
- Allow the child short breaks as needed. Getting up and walking around for a few minutes reduces restlessness and can work wonders in clearing the mind.
- Monitor attention level and be ready to redirect the child's focus when attention wanders.
- Praise the efforts, not just the results. (Do this a lot!)
- Check the completed work.
- Gather all assignments and supplies needed for school the next day. Put everything in the school bag and place it by the front door or other designated location, ready for the morning routine the next day.

- Do something fun and relaxing together after study time and homework is completed.

The Dinnertime Routine

- When possible, schedule a regular family dinner-time.
- Have the child assist in preparing the meal, and cleaning up after it, by assigning age-appropriate tasks.
- Keep dinner conversation pleasant. Save discussions about work, school or family problems for another time.
- Keep the TV off.

The School Night Bedtime Routine

- Cue the child five or ten minutes before the start of the bedtime routine.
- Turn off the TV or computer. Put away toys.
- Allow the child to have a healthy snack if hungry.
- Select and lay out all clothing for the next day
- Bathe, brush teeth, put on pajamas and get into bed.
- Read a book together or talk. The goal is for the child and the parent to unwind from the day.
- Good night kiss. Lights off. Sweet dreams!

CHAPTER 12

Succeeding In College With ADHD

STARTING COLLEGE CAN BE challenging for many individuals with ADHD for one simple reason: the structure that was in place at home and at their high school is suddenly all gone. Unless they have mastered basic organization and time management skills – and, crucially important, *actually use them* – people tend to struggle with developing and maintaining any kind of consistency in their academic work. They are then surprised and disappointed to see that first semester grades are far below what they expected and were used to getting in high school.

In my psychology practice I became used to seeing college students in the second semester of their freshman year. These were not lazy, irresponsible, or unmotivated students. For the most part they were simply inconsistent and unproductive after the initial excitement of starting college wore off. They did not suddenly forget how to be good students, but for various reasons stopped doing the things that made them academically successful in high school.

Managing ADHD in college is not fundamentally different than managing ADHD at any other stage in a person's life. It is fundamentally still about developing the right strategies that feel comfortable for that particular person, and then using those strategies and sticking with them. What is different about college, which applies to all college students, is that for the first time in most peoples' lives it requires a high level of independence and self-regulation. College students with ADHD in particular need to be more conscious about the self-regulation part.

Having ADHD does not preclude doing well academically at *any* level of education. I have worked with many students who did very well in many different academic settings and under a variety of circumstances. ADHD management strategies that are discussed below have worked equally well at local community colleges and private Ivy League schools, in undergraduate programs and in graduate programs such as law school, medical school, business school, and many other fields of study.

It is worth noting once again the simple fundamental fact – people with ADHD are all unique individuals, with a unique set of strengths, weaknesses, and interests. If you are one of those individuals who is currently in school, find the strategies that fit your needs and work best for you. Develop your own system, then use it and stick with it. The tools and resources available to you as a college student are light years beyond the Dr. Pepper and No-Doz strategy discussed in Chapter 1.

Get Your Personalized ADHD Management Plan In Place

If you are a high school student, before even starting college it is a good idea to work with your parents, and perhaps with a counselor at school, to plan a strategy and put it in place. Some important questions to consider:

- *Do you plan to request academic accommodations?* If so, decide what types of accommodations might be helpful for you, and get the process started early (see the following section for more specifics).

- *Will you be taking medication while at school?* If so, work out the details with your medical professional. If you take medication get it right, in terms of finding the most effective medication and most effective dosage level for you (see Chapter 4, "Medication Management and ADHD").

- *Will you have an ongoing support system at school?* If you are working with a therapist or counselor, will you continue with your local counselor or find someone new at school who would be more convenient to work with? If you are taking medication, will you renew prescriptions with your local health care provider or find a new one at school?

- *Will you be needing any kind of tutoring services at school?* Many schools are very good at providing tutoring services for their students, either to address specific academic subjects (e.g., Calculus) or to help with developing specific skills (e.g., study skills, writing skills).

Request Academic Accommodations If You Need Them

Academic accommodations should be requested with no reservation if they would be helpful for a particular student. The goal is always to learn most efficiently, and to demonstrate what you're learning most accurately and efficiently. Accommodations should always be specific to address the needs of the individual student. Some of the most common accommodations include:

- *Extended time testing.* A test or exam should measure what you know – *not* how fast you can get through a test. They are meant to be tests of knowledge, not tests of speed.

  o Distractibility slows down processing speed (for everyone). Excessive distractibility slows down processing speed excessively.

  o The more distractible a person is, the more likely that the distractibility will slow the person down when taking a test or exam.

  o A person who is highly distractible (for example, many people with ADHD) will often struggle to complete all test items within the regular allocated time for that test. This provides an inaccurate measure of the person's knowledge.

  o Extended time testing provides additional time for the person to complete the entire test, and more accurately demonstrates their knowledge and mastery of the material.

o Time and a half (1.5 time) is usually adequate for most people who need extended time. Some students need double time (2.0 time).

o Extended time testing, if needed, should also be requested when taking long standardized tests such as the GRE, LSAT, MCAT, GMAT, and so on.

- *Alternate test location.* Some people need to take exams in a less distractible environment than the usual lecture hall or classroom. An alternate test location accommodation allows them to take the test in a smaller and quieter office, for example, that helps reduce external distractions.

  o Extended time testing and an alternate test location accommodations are very frequently provided together.

- *Copy of instructor's notes.* Getting a copy of the instructor's lecture notes before the lecture allows a student to focus more on the lecture, and less on note taking. Taking notes on the instructor's notes also makes note taking easier. Reviewing the instructor's notes prior to the lecture often makes it easier to follow along with the lecture.

- *Recording a lecture.* Some students find it helpful to record a lecture (with the instructor's permission) and review the recording at a later time. Reviewing the recording is a time-consuming strategy and should be used sparingly.

Optimize Your Learning Strategies

Everyone learns differently. Some people need absolute quiet (or close to it), some do better with background noise. Some study better in the morning, in the afternoon, or even in late evening. Some prefer scheduling longer periods of time, some need short study time blocks and frequent breaks. What works best for you is what works for you.

- *Schedule study times when your mind is most alert.* Some people are morning people, some are night people – and it's based primarily on their biology. Study most efficiently when your mind is most focused.

- *Find one or more optimal study locations.* Some people study best in the library, some in their dorm room or apartment, some at Starbucks. Have one or more go-to locations where you study best – and when you need to focus well, go there.

- *Structure your study schedule to fit your focusing ability.* Some people are most productive when they schedule a two-hour or three-hour study time (with short breaks). Some people study best for 30 to 60 minutes, then take a longer break. Structure your study times to fit your focusing ability.

Basic Organization - Organize Stuff

Even living in a dorm room or sharing an apartment requires a simple organizational system to keep track of things, not constantly misplace things, and avoid having things get buried in piles. Everyone has their own comfort level for how organized they want to be, but also everyone has a minimal need for organization so their environment does not become chaotic.

Minimal organization is necessary to prevent aggravation and wasting time looking for things that tend to get misplaced. Know where your keys are supposed to go, and always put them there. Keep things you work with frequently handy and out in the open. Maintain "clutter-prevention" habits and you won't need to deal with clutter as an ongoing problem.

Clutter-prevention strategies are discussed in detail in Chapter 8 ("De-clutter Your Environment").

Basic Organization - Organize Time and Tasks

One of the biggest challenges facing new college students is learning how to manage time and follow a realistic, balanced schedule. All the structure and schedules of high school and home life are gone. All that free time between classes can make it seem like planning a schedule is no longer necessary.

It may sound paradoxical, but having more free time makes it even more important to plan well. A perception of too much free time makes it easier to put things off, get distracted, and procrastinate. Not scheduling study times makes it easy to fall behind with assigned reading. Not planning time to work on a paper or other project practically guarantees that it will turn into a rush job the night before.

Chapter 9 ("Time Management, Planning, and Prioritizing") discusses strategies for managing time and tasks in more detail.

Practice Anti-Procrastination Strategies On A Daily Basis

Procrastination is the bane of many college students, with or without ADHD. The biology of ADHD makes procrastination more likely, which makes it even more important to develop strategies to fight and reduce procrastination. ("Reduce" is a more realistic and achievable goal than "eliminate" – procrastination is a stubborn and tough beast to kill).

Anti-procrastination strategies are discussed in detail in Chapter 6 ("Get Going! Reducing Procrastination"). The topic is too complicated to cover in this section, and there are no short cuts or simple solutions. This is however a battle that must be fought and won, otherwise college will be a more difficult and less enjoyable experience.

Four Lifestyle Behaviors That Make ADHD Worse

Healthy lifestyle behaviors make a difference – not only in terms of overall health, but also in terms of attention and focusing ability, mood, energy level, and memory functioning. The opposite is also true – unhealthy lifestyle factors cause damage in all those areas. Based on the experiences of many college students with ADHD, the lifestyle factors discussed below can have either a profound positive impact or negative impact. Each behavior is a matter of personal choice.

- *Sleep deprivation.* Many college students are sleep deprived. People stay up late, don't follow any kind of regular sleep schedule, pull all-nighters to study for exams or write papers, etc. Bad for everyone, but even worse for students with ADHD.

- *Low blood sugar level.* Not eating meals on a regular basis leads to low blood sugar levels, which is very bad for concentration, mood, memory, etc. In particular it is not a good idea to skip breakfast or lunch.

- *Lack of exercise.* Aerobic exercise increases levels of all neurotransmitters; including dopamine, serotonin, and norepinephrine (see Chapter 3, "Multimodal Management of ADHD"). Hello improved attention, mood, and energy level. Lack of exercise deprives people of those benefits.

- *Regular marijuana use.* Based again on the experiences of many college students with ADHD, regular marijuana use can have detrimental effects on attention, concentration, activation, and memory functioning.

Has Anyone Yet Told You That These Are......

.... the "best years of your life?" Oh, they have not? Just wait a while, they will.

Whether or not the college years actually turn out to be the best years of *your* life still depends on many, many things that have yet to happen in your life. What is true however is that many people look back on their college years fondly as a time of new freedoms and experiences. It is a time of learning and of personal growth. It is a time that requires hard work, but also allows for more free time and flexibility compared to what comes later in the world of full-time jobs.

Of course these nostalgic remembrances apply best to what is considered the traditional four-year (or five-year) undergraduate college program experience. Many college students pursue their studies on a part-time basis, often while working full time, and often while also parenting and managing family life in the process.

Regardless of the circumstances, a desire to learn and to grow makes college a much more interesting and enjoyable experience. The value of this positive mindset applies to everyone of course, but in my experience it is even more important for students with ADHD.

CHAPTER 13

Finding a Job That Works For You

THERE IS NO SUCH thing as the "perfect" job or career for people with ADHD. Adults with ADHD vary tremendously in terms of interests, abilities, and talents. What makes a job or career a good fit or bad fit depends on many qualities unique to that person, and *not* on whether or not they have ADHD. Looking for a "good ADHD job" is like chasing unicorns.

When it comes to making career or job decisions my advice is the same for everyone. Start with finding the best match between what interests you and what you do well. That might take some thought and honest self-assessment, but it is time very well spent. Consider these basic questions:

- **What interests you strongly?** This question is relevant for everyone, but is particularly relevant and important for people with ADHD.

o It is much easier to focus and stay focused on things that are interesting to you (see Chapter 5, "Pay Attention!").

o It is much easier to get going and not procrastinate on tasks that are naturally interesting to you (see Chapter 6, "Get Going!").

o What might be interesting for Jim or Karen depends entirely on Jim and Karen, and has nothing to do with whether or not they have ADHD.

• **What are your strengths?** Every person has their own unique strengths and weaknesses. It is important to be aware – and honest – about both.

o Doing what comes easier for you, because of your unique talents, makes the work easier. Are you good at communicating with and relating to people? Are you good at building things? Are you a good artist? Without exception, it is always a good idea to maximize one's talents.

o We all have areas of weakness that are unique to us as individuals. Be honest in your assessment of what those are, and be realistic about how much of a drawback those areas of weakness would be to you in a certain job or career. How hard are you willing to work to overcome them, if indeed they can be overcome?

- **What are your values?** Values, in this context, refer to activities or causes that are important and meaningful to you. These provide a sense of satisfaction and accomplishment that comes simply from being involved in them. Are you interested in improving education for underprivileged children? Are you interested in preserving wildlife habitats and protecting our environment?

    o Doing work that is meaningful to us makes the work much easier, and also much more rewarding. It provides a sense of accomplishment. It gives purpose to even the most routine aspects of a job.

    o Doing work that has no meaning or sense of purpose (for you) often results in going through the motions in order to collect a paycheck. Of course there is nothing wrong with working to collect a paycheck, however if given a choice most people would prefer doing work that is personally meaningful.

The point being made that individual differences are paramount in finding a job or career that works for *you*, are there some job characteristics that are more likely to be a "good fit" for people with ADHD biology? Generally speaking the answer is yes, although certain of these characteristics are more relevant for some individuals than others. Also the characteristics are not unique to any particular career or job category.

"Better Fit" Job Variables

- *Interesting, meaningful, and challenging.* Interesting and meaningful are primary and are discussed in detail in the section above. A job that is not sufficiently challenging (e.g., too easy) gets boring very quickly – and boring is the Kryptonite for ADHD.

- *Involves a variety of tasks and responsibilities.* Doing the same thing over and over gets old very quickly. Variety is generally preferable.

- *Social component.* For some people, working directly with other people makes the work more interesting and enjoyable. As opposed to, for example, sitting at a desk doing paperwork.

- *Physically active.* For some people, particularly those who are physically restless or hyperactive, being able to move around is important. They tend to prefer "outside sales" as opposed to "inside sales," for example.

- *Allows for creativity.* Creativity is fun, and many people with ADHD enjoy it and are good at it. A job that allows for creative and innovative contributions is more enjoyable and rewarding.

- *Has some growth potential.* Learning and growing in a job is rewarding for everyone. Feeling stuck and getting stale in a job is likely to happen quicker for a person with ADHD.

- *Opportunity for travel.* Some people find a bit of work travel enjoyable. It creates variety and opportunities to see new places and try new things.

- Work from home opportunities. For many people the opportunity to work remotely one or two days per week is an important factor. Many people find it easier to reduce distractions and focus more efficiently on their work when working from home.

"Worst Fit" Job Variables

- *Work is too repetitive.* Hello, boredom.

- *Over-structured.* A job that does not allow for some autonomy and creativity can eventually feel stifling. These become the jobs that people tend to hate.

- *Highly distracting environment.* This is usually a detriment for people who are naturally distractible. Sometimes there are opportunities to modify the work environment, and sometimes there are not.

- *Micro-manager or critical boss.* These types of bosses and supervisors are found in all industries and fields of work. They are universally disliked for obvious reasons.

  o People with ADHD tend to have a particularly difficult time dealing with them, not least because of heightened emotionality, quick irritability, and heightened sensitivity to criticism.

o A toxic supervisor-employee relationship is one of the main reasons people quit their jobs.

Should I Disclose ADHD at Work?

This is a complicated question that has personal and legal implications. It might well be worthwhile to discuss the particulars of your situation with an attorney with expertise in disability law.

Experts in the ADHD field frequently answer this question as a "no" – *unless* you need to request specific workplace accommodations and can make a good case for them. The problem is that people (including employers) do not always behave in a reasonable and constructive manner. This is complicated by all the negative stereotypes and misconceptions about ADHD (see Chapter 2, "What Is ADHD?").

In my experience, some employers are more enlightened and will respond in a constructive and helpful manner. Some employers will react out of ignorance and may feel threatened by your disclosure, with possible negative ramifications for your job.

Very often it is easier to request helpful changes without bringing up ADHD at all. If, for example, your desk is located in a noisy location, simply ask to move to a less distracting location "because it will help me work better." A good employer will work with you on those kinds of issues whether or not ADHD is a factor.

CHAPTER 14

Tone Down Impulsivity and Hyperactivity

IMPULSIVITY AND HYPERACTIVITY ARE common behaviors for approximately 70% of people with ADHD. The intensity of the biology varies. Degrees of hyperactivity range from fidgeting, to physical restlessness, to being constantly on the go "as if driven by a motor." Being very impatient while waiting in line, or while driving in traffic, or finishing other people's sentences before they are completed, are common examples of hyperactive and impulsive behavior.

The intensity of the impulsivity also varies widely from person to person. For some it means occasionally blurting things out without first thinking about what you want to say. For others it might be excessive interrupting and "talking over" other people that causes communication problems and even relationship problems.

Both hyperactivity and impulsivity need to be understood as pure biology, not related to personality, intelligence, maturity, or any other such factors. Neither is volitional behavior. When they happen they just – happen.

As was previously noted in Chapter 2 ("What Is ADHD?"), hyperactivity and impulsivity are the two aspects of ADHD biology that often get milder with age. Many children who are hyperactive and impulsive are noticeably less so by the time they reach late adolescence or early adulthood.

On the continuum of ADHD biology those individuals who are highly hyperactive and impulsive as children are likely to remain so for their entire lives. It is worth stating once again – ADHD is biology, it is not an illness, and it does not "go away."

Some people find medication helpful in decreasing the intensity of hyperactivity and impulsivity. All people benefit from following a consistent aerobic workout program. Exercises that help calm down the brain, for example meditation and Mindfulness techniques can help to some degree. Many individuals with high levels of hyperactivity however find that they lack the patience to practice meditation. What works much better for them is to go out for a run.

Impulsivity is more conducive to being managed via behavioral strategies than is hyperactivity, and will be the focus for the remainder of this chapter. I make a distinction between three categories of impulsive behavior: behavioral, verbal, and cognitive

Behavioral Impulsivity ("Act Before You Think")

It is a misconception that people with ADHD "don't learn from experience." That is pure nonsense. The problem is not that people don't learn lessons from past experience, but rather that in the moment they simply don't think about those lessons or about the consequences of what they are about to do. This is the essence of impulsivity.

Impulsive people act before they think. Steve knows very well that he is spending too much money on internet shopping, and that his bank account was overdrawn last month. He gave himself a budget for this month. While he is browsing through a collection of casual shirts he comes across one that he *really* likes, and next thing you know he is clicking on the "Make Purchase Now" button. In that moment he does not think about his bank account or his budget – in the moment those things do not exist.

Any kind of reminder cue in that situation might help by jolting a thought of "think first." Flashing a big red mental **STOP** sign in the front of his mind before clicking on the "Make Purchase Now" button might do it. **STOP** – and **THINK**. Delaying every non-essential purchase for a day, to give himself time to think it over, check his budget, etc., would also help.

Verbal Impulsivity ("Speak Before You Think")

The most common type of impulsive behavior is verbal. This leads to frequently interrupting people in conversations, for example. While Sandy is saying something to Lisa a *great* and *really interesting* idea just pops into Lisa's head, and – bam! – Lisa blurts it out. Lisa might be excited about her idea, but chances are that Sandy is none too pleased. If Lisa's intrusive behavior happens frequently Sandy might well consider it inconsiderate and aggravating.

One strategy that might help reduce the impulsivity of intrusive talk is to treat a conversation as a verbal tennis match. You say something (serve). Now wait for the other person to say something (volley). Your turn again to say something else (serve). Wait for the reply (volley).

There is only one verbal tennis ball, you take turns hitting the ball, and you always wait for the person to *finish* their volley before you can serve again. You do not ever serve another ball *before* the other person has completed their volley – that is simply against the rules and very bad manners besides.

Verbal impulsivity also accounts for those embarrassing "oops, did I really just say that?" moments. You know, those unthinking forehead-slapping moments that you wish you could have back. Almost everyone does it on occasion; people with ADHD do it more.

Cognitive Impulsivity ("Decide Before You Think")

What I call cognitive impulsivity involves making snap decisions without planning or thinking it through. Agreeing to work on a charity event for your local zoo – when your schedule is already packed – is one example. Guessing at answers on an exam is another.

Cognitive impulsivity leads to "jump to yes" behavior that causes so many problems for people with ADHD. It is a major reason for why people get overwhelmed. Someone makes a suggestion or an invitation, which sure sounds like a worthwhile cause, and the person immediately jumps to "sure, let's do it!"

CHAPTER 15

ADHD and Addictions

THE LIFETIME OCCURRENCE OF substance abuse problems among adults in the general population is approximately 25%. One in four people are likely to have a problem with substance abuse or addiction at some point in their lives. This includes abuse of alcohol, recreational drugs, and prescription medications.

In comparison, the lifetime occurrence of substance abuse among adults with ADHD is approximately 50%. The risks double. There are many reasons to account for this, however two general reasons come up again and again.

The first reason is that adults with ADHD are more likely to self-medicate, particularly so when they lack awareness or understanding of their ADHD biology and have not yet learned how to manage it well. The second general reason is that many adults with ADHD are drawn to thrill-seeking and novel experiences. As one individual described it very succinctly, he liked to "play with my brain."

An addiction problem is best diagnosed via a professional evaluation from a qualified addictions counselor. Some of the basic signs of addiction include:

- *Strong and urgent cravings for the substance or behavior.* These might include physical cravings (alcohol, cocaine) or emotional cravings (gambling, playing a video game), or both.

- *Loss of control over consumption.* This is why one drink becomes seven, and 30 minutes of video games turns into five hours (or all night long).

- *Continued use in spite of negative consequences.* Sometimes this involves very strong denial (e.g., "I don't have a drinking problem"), but oftentimes individuals are very aware of the problems caused by their addictive behaviors and do them anyway.

- *Inability to cut down despite the desire to do so.* When this is the case, it is time to call in the cavalry and see a counselor or therapist who specializes in working with people with addictions.

Problems with substance abuse and addictions must always be treated seriously. They wreck physical and emotional health, break up families, lose jobs, and cause severe financial problems. In some cases they become life-threatening.

Treatment for substance abuse and addictions is best done by working with an addictions counselor. This may involve outpatient counseling, but sometimes might require a more intense inpatient or residential program. There are also a variety of no-cost support groups found in many communities that focus on a wide variety of chemical and behavioral addictions.

When substance abuse and addictions co-occur with ADHD, in my experience most often the substance abuse is the more serious issue. It is beyond the scope of this book to discuss treatment for substance abuse and addictions. There are people who specialize in substance abuse treatment, but I am not one of them. I always refer people struggling with addictions to the addictions specialists.

My advice to everyone living with substance abuse or addiction is always the same: **see a substance abuse/addictions counselor and get a substance abuse evaluation**. Your life and health, and the lives and health of those you love, may depend on it.

Below is a brief review of some chemical, behavioral, and food addictions. Although these are problems common to all people, in light of the heightened risks for addictions among adults with ADHD awareness of these potential problems becomes even more important.

Chemical Addictions

Stimulants

Many adults with ADHD self-medicate with large amounts of caffeine on a daily basis. Some self-medicate with nicotine via cigarette smoking or vaping. Some people abuse their prescribed stimulant medications. Other stimulants that are abused include cocaine, crystal meth, MDMA (Ecstasy), and ephedrine. All pose serious health risks (yes, including caffeine in large amounts), and some have fatal consequences.

It is not at all surprising that stimulants are the drug of choice for many people with ADHD. All stimulants have the effect of "waking up the brain," which improves alertness and can promote a feeling of calmness. Some drugs such as cocaine, crystal meth, and MDMA also produce feelings of euphoria.

The temporary "benefits" from these drugs are limited and far outweighed by the serious risks to health and life. People who self-medicate often do so out of desperation however. They often lack the knowledge and awareness to make better choices. The most severe case that I am aware of involved a woman who developed an addiction to crack cocaine, because the only way she knew of to overcome her activation difficulty and get herself to start doing housework was to smoke crack cocaine. That is behavior borne of intense desperation.

Any person with ADHD who chooses to use medication to help manage their ADHD should do so with the advice and guidance of their medical professional (see Chapter 4, "Medication Management and ADHD"). The stimulant medications, when used properly, are more effective and safer than the drugs of abuse discussed above. If you're going to medicate yourself, do it right and do it safely.

When taken as prescribed, by mouth, in prescribed doses, the stimulants are generally considered among the safest of psychotropic medications. It is also true however that stimulant medications prescribed for ADHD can be and sometimes are abused.

If stimulant medications are abused, for example taking them in very high doses above what is prescribed, they can become addictive. They *are* addictive if they are abused by crushing and snorting a stimulant tablet or capsule, or if they are crushed and then injected intravenously. How they are taken into the body makes all the difference when it comes to addiction potential. To be used safely the medications must *only* be taken orally and in prescribed doses.

If there is a risk for abusing stimulant medications, there are some choices which make it possible to reduce the risks. The methylphenidate based stimulant Concerta comes in a gel-filled capsule that makes it problematic to be snorted or injected intravenously. The medication Vyvanse (lisdexamfetamine) must be in the gut to be active, which similarly makes it less conducive to be abused.

Alcohol

Alcohol use is part of the culture in many countries around the world. When used in moderation it can enhance certain life experiences such as dining and social functions. When used in excess it becomes highly addictive. Alcohol addiction is considered as severe as heroin addiction.

People self-medicate with alcohol for many different reasons. It is often the self-medicating drug of choice for individuals experiencing symptoms of depression or anxiety. For people with ADHD, no different from anyone else, alcohol can produce a temporary boost in mood and a sense of physical calmness.

Marijuana

Marijuana is approaching a level of social acceptance to rival that of alcohol, although it still remains illegal in many states and other parts of the world. It is used by many people to promote a sense of calmness and relaxation. It is sometimes prescribed for medicinal uses, for example to reduce nausea associated with some cancer treatments. When smoked it may cause damage to the lungs and cardiovascular system.

There are many different strains of marijuana that produce different effects for different people. Some adults with ADHD who are hyperactive believe that it helps tone down their hyperactivity. Some enjoy the pleasant "high" that they get from the drug. This recreational drug, for many people, often falls within the "play with my brain" category.

Adults with ADHD who consider using marijuana should also be aware that regular use can have a negative impact on attention, memory functioning, and activation difficulty. In other words, regular marijuana use could potentially exacerbate problems associated with distractibility, forgetfulness, and procrastination.

The federal agency Centers for Disease Control and Prevention (CDC) reports that approximately 10% of marijuana users develop an addiction to marijuana. Although the addiction is primarily psychological, not physiological, like any other addiction it can cause problems for the individual.

Opiates

Opiate drugs include heroin, morphine, and codeine. In the past several years the abuse of opioid prescription medications (e.g., Vicodin, OxyContin, Percocet), commonly prescribed as pain relievers, has become a national epidemic resulting in many thousands of deaths.

More than 10,000,000 adults in the U.S. abuse prescription pain relievers, according to 2018 government statistics. This is more than twice the number that misuse prescription tranquilizer medication or prescription stimulant medication. These are highly addictive drugs and deadly when abused, causing more than double the number of deaths due to overdosing compared to heroin overdosing. These highly lethal drugs should never be abused.

Sedatives and Tranquilizers

Prescription sedatives and tranquilizers act as central nervous system depressants. The biological brain effect is basically the opposite of that caused by stimulant medications. They are commonly prescribed for anxiety, tension, and sleep disorders (e.g., Xanax, Valium, Ativan, Klonopin, Ambien, Lunesta).

The higher risks for addiction and abuse for some people with ADHD is related to their problems with falling asleep and staying asleep. When the medications are prescribed as sleep aids, continued long term use can lead to addiction. Tolerance can develop, meaning that larger doses are needed to get the same effect. Withdrawal symptoms may occur if the dosage is lowered or the medication is discontinued abruptly.

Hallucinogens

The hallucinogens include LSD, mescaline, psilocybin ("magic mushrooms"), PCP, and DMT. These are powerful mind-altering drugs that can produce hallucinations, severe mood alterations, and changes in reality perception. They are sometimes used as "play with my mind" drugs, but elevated to a reckless and oftentimes danger-ous degree.

The man-made hallucinogens, LSD and PCP, are the most powerful and also most dangerous. LSD use may cause long-lasting changes in brain functioning that last a life-time. PCP was originally developed as an anesthetic, but was discontinued for use with humans due to severe side effects. It is still sold as a street drug. It can cause severe mental health problems, and in large doses can be life-threatening.

Behavioral Addictions

Behavioral addictions tend to get less attention than chemical addictions. Like all addictions however they can cause severe problems in people's lives. They need to be treated seriously, and when necessary treated via profes-sional help.

Internet Addictions

Internet addictions include excessive use of internet me-dia, including social media, message boards, and brows-ing one's favorite websites. But wait, some will say, you just described modern life! Actually, no. What makes it an addiction is excessive use that causes problems in the person's life.

The internet is designed to be distracting and addictive. It is based on immediate gratification. A simple search tells you anything you want to know, and takes you all over the world. There is an endless variety of entertain-ment, information, and social connections. "Hello there," says the ADHD brain, "where have you been all my life?"

One of the reasons your smart phone is so distracting, and you end up checking it multiple times per day, is possibly because you are feeding your internet addiction. The urge to check your Facebook page, or e-mail, or favorite message board, or favorite news site, is too powerful to resist. This is how addictions work.

If the behavior happens so frequently that you are failing to get important work done, or end up hurting the people you love, then it must be acknowledged that a problem exists. After the acknowledgement comes action to remedy the problem.

The only effective solution for an addiction is to abstain. In the case of being constantly distracted by your smart phone, for example, make it a point to put it away when you are working ("out of sight, out of mind"). Only check it during lunch break or other scheduled breaks. Same thing during meal times, or watching a TV show with your family. If you cannot do this by yourself, it may be helpful to talk to someone about it.

Gambling Addictions

Gambling addictions are among the most powerful and destructive behavioral addictions. Whether this involves sports gambling, casino gambling, or other forms of gambling, they often cause severe disruptions in people's lives. Financial problems, relationship problems, and chronic major stress follow. There are no other solutions to a gambling addiction except to get help for it if necessary, and then abstain.

Shopping Addictions

For many people, with or without ADHD, shopping provides a bit of instant gratification and a temporary mood boost. Internet shopping makes it even more convenient. Just bought something on Amazon? Their algorithms immediately present you with several other choices that are likely to intrigue you.

Many people with ADHD are at higher risk for over-spending and for shopping addictions for two major reasons. One, people who are naturally impulsive make the best impulsive shoppers. And two, not keeping track of finances makes it very easy to lose track of how much money a person is actually spending, and thus to not place limits on spending.

Sexual Addictions

By definition a sexual addiction involves a loss of control over one's sexual behavior. For some people this may involve having "serial affairs," whether or not the person is engaged in a committed relationship. For some it involves soliciting sexual partners online, or making frequent use of prostitutes. The most common form of sexual addiction is addiction to pornography.

Addiction specialists tell us that behaviors associated with sexual addictions are not driven by a strong interest in sex, any more than bulimic behavior is driven by a strong interest in food. Often the person is using excessive sexual behavior as a way of dealing with anxiety, stress, loneliness, or other emotional issues.

As with any addiction, sexual addictions cause problems and may require professional intervention. A person who cannot resist the urge to watch internet porn while at work, for example, is at risk for losing his job. A person engaging in serial affairs is putting her health, as well as the health of her spouse or partner, at risk.

Food Addictions

Food addictions may be considered to be both physical and behavioral addictions. They are so common that many people simply regard them as part of their regular eating habits.

Unfortunately the foods that are most addictive are also the foods that are most unhealthy for you. A steady diet of them not only increases risk for obesity and physical illnesses such as diabetes, but also wreaks havoc with mood regulation and cognitive functioning as blood sugar levels take a roller-coaster ride.

Highly processed foods such as cookies and cakes are addictive for the same reasons that addictive drugs are addictive – they deliver a high dose (in this case, of sugar) and have a rapid rate of absorption. That "sugar high" you feel after a bowl of ice cream is an actual, real high. That "carbohydrate craving" you feel is a real craving for carbs. Strong cravings are a primary symptom of addiction.

A research study on food addictions came up with a list of the "top ten" most addictive foods. This list should come as no surprise to anyone:

- Chocolate
- Ice cream
- French fries
- Pizza
- Cookies
- Chips
- Cake
- Popcorn (buttered)
- Cheeseburger

- Muffins

What do these foods have in common, other than being the most popular junk foods and snack foods? They are high sugar, high fat, and highly processed. In moderation (in frequency and volume) they can be tasty treats. In excess they are a nutrition disaster.

When does simple eating become a food addiction? As with any addiction, when the behavior is causing problems and is out of control. Important factors to consider that suggest addictive behavior:

- *Loss of control over volume of consumption.* When having a cup of ice cream leads to eating the entire pint, there may be a problem. Same for eating half of a large pizza, the entire bag of chips, etc.

- *Continuing unhealthy eating habits despite negative consequences.* When a person is significantly overweight (a BMI over 30 is considered obese), or having health problems such as hypertension or diabetes, but still cannot stop eating addictive foods, there is a problem.

- *Inability to stop unhealthy eating even when having the desire to do so.* Making an effort to change unhealthy behavior, and being unable to do it by yourself, is a primary defining characteristic of addictive behavior. This is when it's time to get some help.

CHAPTER 16

Self-Esteem and ADHD: Breaking the Negativity Cycle

ONGOING CRITICISM AND NEGATIVE stereotypes about ADHD take a terrible toll on self-esteem over the years. By "ongoing" I mean starting as early as kindergarten for many children, particularly if they are hyperactive and impulsive. Sit still! Pay attention! Try harder! How many times do I have to tell you..... etc., etc.

By age 10 or 12 many children with ADHD internalize the belief that "I'm a bad kid." Children pick up cues from the behavior of important people in their lives, particularly authority figures such as parents and teachers. No one has to actually say "you're a bad kid" – frequent and repeated messages of frustration, reprimand, and sometimes anger and punishment are enough to drive home that message.

By the time people reach their teen years a pervasive sense of helplessness, and sometimes inadequacy, becomes ingrained. "I'm lazy" and "I'm stupid" are common self-critical messages that become part of the internal self-talk that always goes on in the back of our minds. When these self-critical messages are repeated internally thousands of times, over time they start to feel natural, familiar, and true. Now the negative beliefs such as "I'm lazy" and "I'm stupid" become part of the person's core identity.

By the time they reach early adulthood many people with ADHD develop a sense of underachievement and pessimism about the future. There is a strong sense of "I'm not where I should be," often accompanied by the crushing belief that "I'll *never* get to where I want to be." At that point it is not uncommon to also see feelings of anxiety (excessive worry) and sometimes depression.

Medication does not change these negative beliefs and feelings. For many people therapy can be helpful. For all people with ADHD it is important to recognize and acknowledge their negative beliefs and feelings, then most importantly to *challenge* and fight them. Don't accept negativity just because it feels familiar and "normal."

Below are some strategies to fight negativity and avoid (or repair) damage to self-esteem.

- *Reject labels and stereotypes.* You are a person – not a diagnosis. What makes an individual Karen or Tom involves a very large number of different factors, 95% or more of which have nothing to do with ADHD.

- o Unfortunately most of the stereotypes about ADHD are negative stereotypes. This is where the disorder-mongers are not doing anyone any good.

- o When I hear a person say "I am ADHD" it is often a sign that he or she is identifying too strongly with the diagnosis. No, you are not ADHD – you are Tom or Karen, who also happens to have ADHD.

- *Change the negative scripts.* Our mental scripts are the internal dialogue (self-talk) that we all have with ourselves. Often they become so familiar that we are scarcely aware of them, although they have a big impact on feelings and behavior.

  - o The negative scripts include common self-critical messages such as "I'm lazy," "I can't get anything done," or "I'm an airhead."

  - o Identify your negative scripts. Awareness is the first step.

  - o *Challenge* your negative scripts, resist them, and dismiss them. If you need to work on behavior, great, that can be productive. The negative scripts serve no useful purpose.

- *Identify and appreciate your strengths.* Negative thinking is focused on faults and failures (real or perceived). Most people tend to overlook their strengths or take them for granted.

o Do an honest assessment of your strengths as well as areas of weakness.

o If you're having difficulty identifying your strengths (a real problem for many people), ask one or two people who know you well for their honest opinions.

o Take pride in your strengths. Appreciate them. Celebrate them.

o Appreciating your strengths is not a sign of boastfulness or arrogance. It is simply a healthy way to balance out the negativity.

• *Don't punish biology, learn to manage it better.* Without exception, getting self-critical about one's biology is unhelpful. It is not your "fault" that you are distractible or forgetful, any more than it is your "fault" that you have brown hair or blue eyes.

o Critical comments about ADHD biology (restlessness, distractibility, forgetfulness, etc.) are especially harmful to children with ADHD. This is inexcusably bad behavior on the part of adults who make them.

o Critical comments about ADHD biology are not helpful for adults with ADHD either.

o ADHD biology needs to be understood in its proper context, and accepted as such. We can change behavior – but we can't change biology.

- *Focus on solutions, not problems.* Negative thinking is always focused on problems. Should have done this, could have done that, can't do this, can't do that -- the list seems endless.

  o Turn that negative script upside down. You already know what the problems are; it is a gigantic waste of time and energy to dwell on them further. Focus instead on the things you *can* do.

  o Set realistic goals and expectations, then get to work on the things you *can* do. This is what produces constructive results and leads to healthy behavior change.

  o We are not prisoners of our past. No one is stuck doing things the same way they have always done them. Doing things differently *does* produce different results.

  o The change from a problems-focused mind-set to a solution-focused mindset is a process that will likely require some time and work. Staying in a problem-focused mindset is much worse.

- *Forgive those who didn't (or still don't) understand.* It is not uncommon for some people with ADHD to wonder about "why didn't my parents understand" or "why didn't my teachers understand?"

  o Those are natural "what if" questions. They don't have any helpful answers.

o We don't know what we don't know. Blaming others for what they did not know does not change history nor help manage the present.

- *Educate (or avoid) those who won't understand.* One of the most frustrating experiences for many individuals with ADHD is when people they care about cannot or will not accept what ADHD is about. That often feels like a very painful and personal repudiation.

    o Some family members, partners, or friends react with some variation of the "I don't believe in ADD" message. That can be infuriating, because *you* certainly believe in it and can see how it affects your life.

    o The centuries-old saying that "you can lead a horse to water, but you can't make it drink," is as true now as it ever was. This of course applies to people as much as horses. If anything, people can be even more stubborn than horses.

    o Talking to people you care about in an honest and open manner is a good idea. Whether or not they are willing to listen is up to them.

    o If a person is so stubborn or so negative that they will not listen or be open to learning, it may be time to stop beating your head against the wall.

CHAPTER 17

Living Happily and Well With ADHD

ONE MORE TIME – ADHD is biology that can be managed well. Millions of people all around the world prove this on a daily basis. They are employed in every occupation you can think of – and yes, I have met many hundreds of them.

People with ADHD are teaching your children at school. They are answering the phone when you call your insurance company. They are featured stars in some of your favorite TV shows and movies. Some are developing and managing businesses that employ hundreds of people. Many are very creative IT people and programmers who keep communications systems running. Some are getting your tax returns done (accurately). Some are providing medical care and doing surgery at the hospital in your community (and being *exceptionally* well focused, even hyperfocused, when they do).

Many people with ADHD make very caring, sensitive, empathetic, and loving partners, spouses, and parents. Many grew up in households that were "chaotic but loving," because one or both of their parents also had ADHD. They strive to provide that love for their own families, while also toning down the chaos to a level more in line with "normal" family chaos.

When it is well understood and managed, ADHD is not a limiting condition in people's lives. It should not stop anyone from achieving their realistic goals – "realistic" meaning that the person has the talent to match their ambition and is willing to put in the necessary work (which is true for all people, ADHD or no ADHD). What works well for managing ADHD depends entirely on the person, their unique strengths and weaknesses, and the specific ways that ADHD biology affects their behavior. Each person is uniquely different.

This book was written with two primary goals in mind. The first is to advance and improve understanding of ADHD beyond the distorted negative stereotypes. In my experience this is an essential first step in getting past the misconceptions relating to ADHD. It is fundamental to understanding and self-acceptance.

The second goal is to present a set of practical strategies to help manage the complicated biology of ADHD. Every one of these strategies has been used successfully by real people in real life. Different people will find different strategies to be more relevant and helpful for them, which is perfectly fine and in fact expected. Let experience guide you in developing strategies and systems that work best for you.

Book Bonus:
Real People, Real ADHD

Merle

ADHD Coach; Community Organizer

I found out I had ADHD eight years ago. I was fifty years old when I subjected myself to a rigorous, multi-hour testing session, and it seemed pointless. I knew I had lots of problems, but there was no way I had ADHD.

I'd been in one form or another of professional therapy most of my life since I was sixteen, spent maybe twenty years attending and leading Twelve-Step meetings, read hundreds of self-help books. Because I already knew so much about mental health, when I accepted a friend's challenge to go back to school to get a Master's in psychology, I knew it'd be a breeze because I'd already been "studying" this stuff all my life. I was familiar with the diagnostic criteria for ADHD. I thought I knew what ADHD was — but I was wrong by a mile.

My mental image of ADHD was, you know, the little boy in grade school that wouldn't sit down and wouldn't be quiet in class. That was not me at all. I was usually good in school, often excellent, and I was polite and very quiet throughout grade school and high school. So quiet actually, that sometimes I would go through the entire school day without uttering one word out loud. When I'd finally open my mouth to say something because I had to, my voice would be hoarse from not using it for so many hours. Ha ha, that is not me anymore! At some point I changed. For the past thirty years or so I've been very talkative. Very verbal.

The only thing I remember hearing about ADHD throughout my entire Master's program came not from a lecture, but from one of my classmates. He'd said his son had ADHD, but later he admitted in class that he too had ADHD. He was a smart guy, maybe one of the smartest students in our cohort. Perhaps he seemed a little "all over the place" in his conversations, but other than that, I couldn't "see" any ADHD in him.

So when my new therapist explained hyperfocus to me, it started to click. Yes, sometimes I could focus so well that I'd be in my own world, oblivious to all external stimuli. People would say things to me, call my name, wave their hands near my face, and I wouldn't hear a thing. That explained why I was able to get my homework done and do so well in school, despite my assignments always being done at the last minute.

Sometimes I'd have maybe a month to work on a research paper or something, and the stress about the project would hang over me like a dark cloud of unfinishedness. Even so, I'd still wait until the night before, finally getting it done in a panicky sleep-deprived state. Then I'd probably wake up late the next day and spend money on a cab to get to class because I wouldn't make it on time if I took the bus.

In the cab on the way to class, my heart would pound with anxiety. If the cab driver missed a light or veered from the most direct route, I'd fall apart. Then, as though this behavior were perfectly reasonable, I'd catch my breath and stroll into class. Whew--just made it! That kind of feeling. Like yanking a rabbit out of a hat because I'd pulled off the impossible. Amazingly, I was a straight-

A student throughout most of my life, with the one notable exception being sixth grade. I got F's in many classes that year, practically needing to be held back.

I don't know what happened with me that year. There's no science behind this observation, but I'm not the first person I know with ADHD who had trouble with sixth grade. I just didn't know what was going on in school. Like if we had a big assignment or a major test due, I'd walk into class saying, "Huh? There's a test today?" Of course, my classmates would look at me like I was an idiot. And at the time it seemed they were right.

The one area I did shine in that year was creative writing class. My teacher thought I had a lot of talent because I was able to share my feelings so well through my writing.

Oh yeah, there was another area of "giftedness" that showed up for me around that time. I loved drawing cartoons and writing little stories. I'd make tiny little "comic books," including sly references to certain students, maybe playfully satirizing something about them, or who they "might" be interested in dating, or maybe the stories would include some silly things about a teacher. My little books would get passed around class. It was maybe the only thing I did during that time that was considered cool. For a very shy girl, I was precociously clever.

My moments of feeling special were fleeting and rare, though. As an adult, I struggled to come across as a somewhat normal person, but my lack of planning and procrastination gave me away. A friend of mine tried to be helpful. She said, "You work best under pressure." But I knew she was wrong. The truth was that I ONLY worked under pressure. For me, deadlines exist so that I can bump up against them, getting as close as I can to them, maybe making a few excuses to extend them just a little bit. It's almost like there's no other way. In my mind, anyway.

I don't know how to arrange my life to not have time commitments and/or deadlines be the enemy. "What time do I need to be at that event?" I'll ask. And then I tell myself that this time I'll arrive comfortably early. I fantasize about maybe stopping at Starbucks to buy a breakfast sandwich and a green tea latte before the event starts, enjoying it for maybe a half-hour before I leisurely stroll over to the meeting or class or job that's in walking distance from the coffee shop. But, alas, it pretty much never happens.

I'm lucky if I even make it to Starbucks in time to get ANYTHING to eat or drink before I have to be some-where. Sometimes I'll just grab it to go and bring it with me, hoping that my "breakfast" (even if it's 2:00 PM) won't be a problem or so conspicuous that everyone just stares at me. Then I'm embarrassed because of my poor planning and I can't pay attention to what's going on an-yway for maybe the first fifteen minutes of whatever it is that I'm there for.

And the really crazy thing is -- I most likely wasn't doing anything important prior to mismanaging my time and leaving the house late. Probably researching something trivial online or playing a video game or doing some oth-er non-essential thing. I just don't understand it. Even now, with all I know about ADHD, and with the help of my stimulant medication every morning, it's still hard for me to understand time management and planning. I feel

I'm just ridiculous in this area. How can I be so smart in some areas and not manage time well? How???

When I found out I had ADHD it was a huge relief! People with ADHD need to be identified early and they may need extra help with things like planning and figuring out which thing to do next. That's why non-medication treatment for ADHD is so essential. There simply aren't enough professionals out there who understand ADHD. Medicine can be helpful -- it has helped me quite a bit -- but medicine can only do so much. Medication won't make decisions for you. It won't help you set priorities. It will help you follow through AFTER you've determined the course of action you need to take.

I'm passionate about ADHD because I knew what it was for years, yet completely missed seeing it in myself. Finding out about it has made a world of difference. I want to devote my energy to helping talented people like me (dare I say it?) become all they were made to be. It's very painful to go through life not understanding how you're wired differently than most people are. To always feel like you're trying to play catch-up with life.

I want to help people get un-stuck and get on with their lives in a more productive way. Currently, I have a daily "talk show" every weekday morning on Zoom now for people with ADHD (or for people without ADHD who happen to like ADHD folks and like the format). It helps me and it helps others by giving us some daily structure.

Bibliography

Brown, T.E. (2017). *Outside the Box: Rethinking ADD/ADHD in Children and Adults.* American Psychiatric Publications.

Hallowell, E.M. & Ratey, J. (2011). *Driven to Distraction (Revised).* Anchor Books.

Ratey, J. & Hagerman, E. (2008). *Spark: The Revolutionary New Science of Exercise and the Brain.* Little and Brown.

Roland, R. & Wright, S. (2005). *Fidget to Focus: Sensory Strategies for Living with ADD.* iUniverse.

Solden, S. (2004). *Journeys Through ADDulthood.* Bloomsbury Publishing.

ADDitude Magazine
www.additudemag.com

ABOUT THE AUTHOR

Peter Jaksa, Ph.D., is a Clinical Psychologist in Chicago, Illinois. He has worked extensively with adults and children with ADHD for the past 35 years, providing diagnostic and therapeutic services. From 1999 to 2001 he served as President of the Attention Deficit Disorder Association (ADDA). Currently Dr. Jaksa serves on the Scientific Advisors Board for *ADDitude Magazine* and is a contributing writer for the magazine.

Books by Peter Jaksa:
Real People, Real ADHD (with Merle Kaplan, M.A.)
Decebal Triumphant
Decebal and Trajan
Decebal Defiant: Siege At Sarmizegetusa

www.addcenters.com

Peter Jaksa

Made in the USA
Monee, IL
13 March 2021